SECRETS
OF THE

Inc.
500

SECRETS
OF THE

Inc.
500

Strategies to Grow Your Business Fast
and Outrun Your Competitors

Advantage®

Published by Advantage, Charleston, South Carolina.
Member of Advantage Media Group.

ADVANTAGE is a registered trademark and the Advantage colophon is a trademark of Advantage Media Group, Inc.

Printed in the United States of America.

ISBN: 978-159932-384-8
LCCN: 2012952831

This publication is designed to provide accurate and authoritative information in regard to the subject matter covered. It is sold with the understanding that the publisher is not engaged in rendering legal, accounting, or other professional services. If legal advice or other expert assistance is required, the services of a competent professional person should be sought.

 Advantage Media Group is proud to be a part of the Tree Neutral® program. Tree Neutral offsets the number of trees consumed in the production and printing of this book by taking proactive steps such as planting trees in direct proportion to the number of trees used to print books. To learn more about Tree Neutral, please visit **www. treeneutral.com**. To learn more about Advantage's commitment to being a responsible steward of the environment, please visit **www. advantagefamily.com/green**

Advantage Media Group is a leading publisher of business, motivation, and self-help authors. Do you have a manuscript or book idea that you would like to have considered for publication? Please visit **www.advantagefamily.com** or call **1.866.775.1696**

TABLE OF CONTENTS

PROLOGUE

Dear Readers,

This book is a departure for us in many ways. In the strictest sense of the word, it is a departure in that it is not our usual modus operandi: not our usual product. I started Advantage Media Group seven years ago because I fundamentally believed the right book could change a person's life forever. I still believe that, as strongly as ever.

This is why we at Advantage Media Group continue to publish books by businesspeople who feel they have a story to tell, a lesson to teach, or a philosophy to impart—and since our inception we have done this more than four hundred times for more than three hundred and fifty authors. That is a lot of wisdom.

As an entrepreneur who started a business, and now as an entrepreneur concerned with growing that same business, I believe reading has the power to change people in a positive way. This brings me to the second sense of "departure." This book is different than every other book Advantage has published—as opposed to the thoughts of one author filling a single volume, it is a collection of thoughts, both general and specific, from several *Inc.* 500 CEOs. We at Advantage hope that anyone who reads this book might also experience a sort of departure of his or her own, and find a new way of thinking.

We hope that by reading this book, and by examining the insight imparted by the leaders of small- and mid-sized businesses, you will find answers to your own pressing business questions—or perhaps to questions you never even thought to ask. It is our wish that this clearinghouse of wisdom will help you fuel your own departure into a new blue sky of thought, inspiration, productivity, and success.

The accounts in this book contain all you need to launch that journey. You might be struck by the way Abhi Rajmane completely changed his lifestyle and business practices following his experience on the way to catch a commuter train outside of Chicago one winter morning. You might be moved by the way Nick Chasinov knew he had found the perfect New Jersey headquarters for his company when he came across a location that had a lake, a courtyard, picnic tables, and a barbecue. Or you might be inspired by the way Blake Fulton and Brad Carlson founded their Missouri-based company in a *college dorm room.*

"Before we got started we believed our age might cause us some problems," Fulton says in this book, "but our own minds were what held us back."

Indeed, our minds are always what hold us back, regardless of our age.

You might want to know about how Vicky Thompson's Georgia business achieved 6,267 percent growth and landed her on the *Inc.* 500 list. You might also be interested in how Bryan Mehr operates his California company in an industry that awards most of its jobs to larger competitors in other U.S. regions. How does he keep his company viable? Not by doing the same thing better than his competitors do, but by doing different things altogether.

As entrepreneurs, we have to be creative, flexible, and eternally curious. This is why this book is such a valuable resource, and, frankly, such a delight to read. It is filled with valuable business lessons from successful entrepreneurs of all ages, who thrive in a variety of industries from coast to coast.

I think entrepreneurs are naturally curious individuals. One of the mantras I have tried to live by is, "Success leaves clues." If you are wise, you will uncover and turn over as many rocks as possible to find those clues. When an opportunity such as this arises—the chance to feature the 500 fastest-growing private companies in America—well, as an entrepreneur who wants to quickly and aggressively grow my company, I would be wrong if I did not try to make the most out of this opportunity. I would be remiss in not trying to figure out what is going on in the minds of the CEOs and other leaders who run these *Inc.* 500 companies. As an entrepreneur, and as the CEO of Advantage Media Group, I thought, "Hey, wouldn't it be fun to turn the tables?

Instead of publishing just one author, we could interview a variety of entrepreneurs and see what makes them tick." I wanted to see what keeps these entrepreneurs up at night, what strategies they employ, what tactics they believe have aided in their success, and what factors have contributed to their massive growth. What clues are these successful people leaving for the rest of us? How can I, as an entrepreneur, use those clues to positively impact my own business?

I firmly believe successful entrepreneurs do not have to invent anything. They just have to be smart enough to see a great idea and mimic it within their own business. McDonald's is No. 1 in its industry, but No. 2 and No. 3—Wendy's and Burger King—are doing just fine. These companies' executives took an idea pioneered by McDonald's and put their own twist on it. Today, they enjoy a huge share of the market.

I think you can pay close attention to what successful people are doing and then figure out a way to duplicate and implement those tactics within your own business—or even within your own life. At its core, this book is a collection of wisdom from some of the nation's smartest, most talented, and successful people: human beings on a quest to do their best, compete passionately, and solve life's most interesting puzzles. This is a book for anyone who is interested in starting a business, growing that business, or developing a more rewarding, enriching, and passionate life.

One of my great heroes is Walt Disney. Unfortunately, he died twenty years before I was born. Even though I never got to work with him, I have been able to implement the magic of Disney in my own business simply by reading books about my hero and his company. If those types of books did not exist, I would never have been able to do that. My business, the team members we employ, and the customers we serve would all have been worse off because we didn't have that knowledge or inspiration.

Books are windows into another world. Through these windows, we can look into some of the greatest minds in history. In terms of business, even though I never had a chance to personally meet Steve Jobs, Albert Einstein, or other great innovators, I can read their books (or books about them) and get to know them. Through reading these books, I feel as though I am having a one-on-one conversation with these inspirational individuals. It is as if they are giving me personal advice that I can immediately implement in my business to make it better. This book reads in exactly that same manner. The wisdom of our contributors is direct, focused, and succinct.

The people we have chosen to feature in this book have some of the most brilliant business minds in America; they call the shots for the country's 500 fastest-growing companies. What are they doing that is different? What are they doing that is unique? How can they be growing by 500 percent a year when the average American business grows by 2 percent?

I hope that when you are done reading this book there are many yellow highlighter marks in it, many dog-eared pages, and a great deal of underlining. If you read it on your Kindle, iPad, or Nook, I hope your version is filled with electronic highlights, notes, and underlining. While this is a book that will certainly entertain you, it is also a book to be *used*.

Our goal and hope is that you find ideas and inspiration that move you, and, more importantly, that you take action—that you take these ideas and implement them in your own business, or life, using them to elevate your methods of operating, living, and being. Whether you are trying to grow a business or live more creatively, passionately, and wisely, the ideas in this book will help take you up to the next level. They will help you with your own departure.

Good reading and good learning to you. Enjoy the journey.

Sincerely,

Adam Witty, CEO
Advantage Media Group
awitty@advantageww.com
advantagefamily.com

Mike Volpe

HubSpot

#33

MIKE VOLPE

CHIEF MARKETING OFFICER, HUBSPOT
CAMBRIDGE, MASSACHUSETTS

Mike Volpe - Hubspot
Rank #33
3-Year % Growth: 6,015%
Revenue: $15.6 Million
Industry: Software
# of Employees: 179
City/State: Cambridge, MA

HubSpot, named for its hometown of Boston, is a pioneer in inbound marketing and has created all-in-one marketing software for more than 7,000 companies in forty-five countries. Stacked with graduates of MIT and other elite Boston-area universities, HubSpot offices are also crammed with the creature comforts and boondoggles of college kids themselves: a refrigerator stocked with beer and snacks, and foosball and ping pong tables just waiting for players. Regardless of how good the employees are at those parlor games, the company is a leader in its field.

WHY DID YOU CHOOSE THIS FIELD?

When we looked around, we saw this huge, fundamental change happening in marketing. The way people bought and researched products was changing, and we felt like most people in marketing weren't adapting to that change. People were still cold-calling, sending out direct mail and different types of spam, and promoting other types of advertising that consumers were increasingly ignoring.

People were still cold-calling, sending out direct mail and different types of spam, and promoting other types of advertising that consumers were increasingly ignoring.

If you look on the buyers' side, they're asking friends for recommendations in social media. They're reading blogs. They're using search engines to find solutions to their problems. Marketers weren't doing an effective job of adjusting their marketing to match the way buyers were behaving. We wanted to help solve that problem and help make marketing better for everyone. Mostly, we wanted to make it more effective for businesses and less obtrusive and annoying to the people receiving it. That was the crux of the idea behind HubSpot and everything that flowed from there. It led us to build a software platform that helps marketers do every aspect of their marketing, but in a more modern, inbound way.

HOW IS IT GOING?

Our growth rate has been more than 6,000 percent. It was not something we expected. We expected to grow fast, and we thought we were in a great market, but we did not expect that level of success as quickly as we got it. It definitely exceeded our expectations.

HOW DID YOU DO THAT?

The first thing responsible for that growth is we were able to recognize a fundamental shift in the market and tap into it. We knew marketing was fundamentally changing because buyers were changing their behavior. Any time there's a shift in a market, forming a company that helps people deal with that shift or change, or even takes advantage of it, usually creates tremendous opportunities.

When Jeff Bezos saw people were starting to buy and sell products on the Internet, he started Amazon, and, obviously, that's become a huge company. There are lots of other examples like that. I think that's probably the primary thing—we were able to tap into the big change happening in marketing.

Any time there's a shift in a market, forming a company that helps people deal with that shift or change, or even takes advantage of it, usually creates tremendous opportunities.

The second key to our growth has been people. I think it's something employers pay lip-service to, but we spend a lot of time on our culture and interviewing. We rate and evaluate folks during the interview process and later, when they're employees, and we try to have a top-notch team so we can execute well. That's the second big thing.

We spend a lot of time on our culture and interviewing.

Third, we've worked hard to maintain a highly scalable, low-cost marketing and sales model. We do the vast majority of our own lead generation through inbound marketing. We've got a rather large sales team, but they don't do any cold-calling. They just follow up on the leads we generate for them in marketing. They're all inside sales folks. It's a little different than the traditional model. I think that's helped us keep costs low, which allows us to funnel money back into the business so we can grow faster. These are the three biggest factors to our growth.

HAVE YOU HAD TO MAKE ANY ADJUSTMENTS RECENTLY?

The big adjustment we made recently is we had a focus on smaller businesses initially, and we had this goal of selling to the small business market. Over the past couple of years, we have also been selling to larger businesses. That's driven our growth a lot, especially in the past year or so. That's definitely been going well. If you look at just the past year, our customer growth was 50 percent, but our revenue growth was more than 80 percent. What that means is, while we're still growing our customer base quickly, we're adding an increasing number of larger companies that are paying more revenue. That's been a key part of our growth that was not there in the first few years.

Today, we have more than 7,000 companies using our software to power their marketing. Four years from now, we hope to have 30,000 companies using our software. I think there's an opportunity for our software to start to become the standard platform designed for the way current marketing should be done. Today, the vast majority of our customers use software for their marketing that HubSpot built and powers.

I think there's an opportunity for our software to start to become the standard platform designed for the way current marketing should be done.

I think the change that's going to happen over the next few years—and it's already starting to happen a little bit this year—is companies are going to build software applications that integrate with and work on top of HubSpot. We have opened up our system to allow that; it's an open system. Fifty other companies have already built their own applications that integrate with HubSpot.

Four years from now, I think people will see HubSpot as the home base, or hub, of their marketing, but they may use more applications from other companies besides HubSpot. These will be applications that are integrated with HubSpot and run within HubSpot almost seamlessly. Just like you can develop an application that works within Facebook without leaving Facebook and build on top of that platform, you can build on our platform. That's where I think the future of our business, our industry, is headed over the next four years.

I think our competition is just starting to awaken to the idea of developing more of a marketing suite. By that, I mean most of our competitors provide individual point solutions. Some of them are acquiring each other and starting to build up more functionality, trying to duplicate our strategy. That's obviously been our strategy from the beginning: to be this all-in-one marketing platform. An open platform that other people can build on top of is something none of our competitors have anything close to right now.

An open platform that other people can build on top of is something none of our competitors have anything close to right now.

DOES WHERE YOU OPERATE MATTER?

We're in Cambridge, Massachusetts, and we are all passionate about Boston. Folks who are from here know the local nickname for this city is "The Hub." And our business is called HubSpot. *HubSpot* means lots of different things. It's the hub for all of your marketing, and we're big on building a large, longstanding company right here in The Hub. We want to be an anchor tenant for the technology industry within Boston. The technology industry got started here, but it's been a little bit on the decline and has lost out, in terms of growth, to Silicon Valley. We think we have an opportunity to start reversing that tide by building a big, successful company here.

The technology industry got started here, but it's been a little bit on the decline and has lost out, in terms of growth, to Silicon Valley.

Our CEO says he wants to build a company that's as big and full of impact, over the years, as something like Hewlett-Packard. There's definitely an aspiration to build more of a Silicon Valley-sized technology industry here in Boston. Most of HubSpot's founding team members are from MIT, and a lot of us have degrees from there. We've been able to hire many smart people, specifically from MIT. Our office is just a few blocks from the MIT campus, as well as being close to Harvard, Boston University, and the other schools here. Our co-founders met at MIT, and our first office was two blocks away from campus.

The key to being successful in our industry is being unique and effective. So many marketing software products all do approximately the same thing. They are all based on the prior generation's ideas of how you should do marketing. I think people are just starting to wake up to this marketing transformation that we were on board with five or six years ago.

Leading the innovation is important to us. Defining the new method of how marketing should be done and implementing that in our software product is the most important thing. I think that's been the corridor to our success to this point—leading the innovation, leading the way—and responding to the transformation that's happening and making it available to our customers through our software product.

The biggest lesson we've learned at HubSpot can be summed up in the words of our co-founder Dharmesh Shah, who says, "It's about releasing early and often." It's about not waiting until whatever you have is totally perfect. It's about putting it out there, getting feedback from your customers and rapidly iterating on that, and making the product better. I think too many entrepreneurs have release anxiety and are unwilling to put their toe in the water or move forward. I think that's something we did a good job at during HubSpot's early days. Often, we would release a product that was in beta. It would not be perfect, but it would certainly help lots and lots of people. I think getting that early start helped us move forward and move quickly.

I think too many entrepreneurs have release anxiety and are unwilling to put their toe in the water or move forward.

WHAT'S YOUR DAILY READING ROUTINE?

I've got an iPad and an iPhone, and I've got Google Reader, Twitter, and Facebook set up, and that's where almost all of my reading comes from. I read a variety of RSS feeds from different marketing blogs and some technology industry blogs. I also read a couple of apps that aggregate my feeds on my iPad. I'm not necessarily tied to a single publication. It's more about aggregation and using my social network as a filtering mechanism. Look at apps like Flipboard, which takes your Twitter followers and a few other topics of interest to you, and bubbles up the things that are the most interesting and having the most impact; that's the kind of reading I do. I use a couple different ones, but those types of applications basically govern most of my reading routine.

I may sound biased, but I think every entrepreneur, especially marketing entrepreneurs, should read a book called *Inbound Marketing,* which our co-founders Brian Halligan and Dharmesh Shah wrote. I think it has become a classic within the marketing industry. It's been translated into a number of different languages. I just saw a Japanese copy floating around the office.

Abhi Rajmane

NABROS Inc.

ABHI RAJMANE

FOUNDER AND PRACTICE PARTNER, NABROS INC.

WARRENVILLE, ILLINOIS

Abhi Rajmane – NABROS Inc.
Rank #361
3-Year % Growth: 940%
Revenue: $2.7 Million
Industry: IT Services
# of Employees: 54
City/State: Warrenville, IL

NABROS Inc. consultants do not watch the clock; at least, not in the traditional way. The company provides fixed-cost consulting services (and a money-back guarantee) in Enterprise Resource Planning implementations, business optimization, re-engineering, turnkey web application development, interfacing/integration, and accounting/auditing to Fortune 500 corporations worldwide, including Butterball, Tellabs, Toyota, RR Donnelley, Harman/Kardon, and Scotts. Rajmane founded NABROS in the suburbs of Chicago in 2002 after he had a life-changing epiphany on his way to the train.

If we talk about our growth rate financially it's been 140 percent. But we measure our growth on planned retention and employee retention, plus increases in innovation in our research and development department. If we were to measure those parameters, we've had 100 percent retention of our clients and 95 percent retention of our team, plus we've had an increase of about 300 percent in new services and products launched in the last three years.

All of those increases exceeded our expectations, both according to our own measurement guidelines and the standard measurement of financial growth. We were anticipating about 80 percent or so growth in each of those categories, considering the global economic situation. But what we saw was an opportunity to grow even more in those market conditions. Our clients were looking for a partner in consulting expertise and IT.

We're in the business of consulting, so customer satisfaction is the most important thing. Managing our clients' expectations and satisfying their needs is our utmost priority, aside from the fact that we have always focused on making things simple. What that entails is removing complications, talking in layman's terms, and making sure the initiative is clear and everyone who is part of a particular project understands what we are trying to do and sell.

Focus is also key. Getting our global team all going in the same direction has been a challenge. I think we're doing a good job of it, especially in terms of ensuring everyone is focused on one key thing, which is making everything simple and delivering the best solution. Our priority, again, is ensuring that we increase our client base and keep our clients satisfied. Our sales team, or rather our business development team at-large, does not focus on the financial aspect of our business, per se. They focus more on how many clients we have, how many clients we have retained, and how many new services we have initiated.

On top of it all, we strive to be fair. We don't have any fine print in our contracts. We use simple contracts and we are easy to do business with. We make an effort to keep things simple, open, and fair. Our growth is primarily due to these factors.

On top of it all, we strive to be fair. We don't have any fine print in our contracts.

HOW DID YOU COME UP WITH THIS PHILOSOPHY?

I learned this from my uncles and grandparents, who ran everything from retail shops to restaurants to hotels. So I cannot take credit for anything new. There have just been these basic fundamentals that we have applied to NABROS and to our billable workforce.

WHY DID YOU CHOOSE THIS KIND OF BUSINESS INSTEAD OF FOLLOWING IN YOUR UNCLES' OR GRANDPARENTS' FOOTSTEPS?

This might take a little bit of time. I like to emphasize this because it's a personal story. I used to work for a company in downtown Chicago. I lived in the suburbs and I used to catch the train and go downtown. One December, I had parked my car at the commuter station and I was running to catch the train. I started losing my breath because of the cold. I got under the tunnel. I wouldn't say it was a frightening moment, but just the fact that I was out of breath was a little scary.

That same month, my father-in-law passed away. When I combined the two events and thought about it, the thinking process gave me a new perspective on life and priorities. So I went back in to this company that I was working for at the time, which was just a phenomenal company, and said, "I want to work from home, or from anywhere in the world that I choose, considering my parents do not live with us here. And if I need to be someplace to take care of them and my family, I need to have a flexible schedule. So, technically, I'll own my time, but I'll do the work and I'll deliver." And the company, being a huge Fortune 500 company, could not justify letting me do this because it had to be included in their policy and it wasn't. Eventually I had to separate myself from them.

When I got back home—this was about ten years ago—I said to my wife, "Okay, what do we do now?" I started off doing body shopping for a month, and then I tried setting up a PC manufacturing unit. And again, one day I woke up and I had that—what would you call it?—just a subtle reminder as to why I got into technology. I asked myself why I did my business management training. It was primarily because when I was a teenager I'd always wanted to help sick companies become healthy and profitable again. The only reason I did that part-time or as an assistant was that most people said it wasn't feasible as a full-blown career.

When I got back home—this was about ten years ago—I said to my wife, "Okay, what do we do now?"

So those were the things that had always interested me. I realized that they had driven me from my education to my experience, which was all in that line. I was helping employers become more efficient and lean, and helping them apply technology with the right perspective. I decided that the first thing we could sell is what we're good at, and that was making everything simple. That's how the company got started. Another important motivator was the ability to work on a flexible schedule from wherever we like, making sure that we could balance life and work better.

Over the last ten years, we believe we have built the foundation and laid the groundwork for the growth we are expecting. We are currently working toward a hundred-year plan. That is how we have phased it: five years, ten years, twenty years, thirty, fifty, and then, subsequently, one hundred. In a year or so, we hope to be in a position to contract investment for expansion. This does not mean we want to go public. We just want to expand in a manner that helps us keep our priorities in focus.

In four years, we will be basically kick-starting our plan to become the number one consulting firm in the world by 2020. That's our step-by-step goal. Technically, we began working toward this in 2010, and we are two years into it. In another four years, we'll have everything in place. At that point, we will kick-start our strategy and put in place the steps that will enable us to become the world's number-one consulting firm.

///

In four years, we will be basically kick-starting our plan to become the number one consulting firm in the world by 2020. That's our step-by-step goal.

///

HOW DO YOU FEEL YOU ARE DOING TODAY ON YOUR WAY TO BECOMING THE WORLD'S BEST?

This brings up another personal story. When I was in the eighth or ninth grade, I was planning to run in a 5-mile race. I practiced for it for two months or so. I timed myself and did everything I could to prepare. I even had the race planned out in my head. On the day of the race, everything was fine. We started the race. It was going well until we got about a mile and a half from the end. One of the guys who always competed with me in school overtook me.

At that juncture, I don't know what happened—it might have been the competitiveness or ego—but I started accelerating. That was not what I had planned, and it was not what I had practiced. Of course, what happened was I let go of my plan and ended up losing the race. Competitiveness had gotten the best of me. But I am glad I lost that race because it taught me a great lesson: to run my own race. If you ask me today how that applies to NABROS, well, we have our own niche. We are the only consulting firm in the world that delivers fixed-cost solutions with a money-back guarantee. We compete with IBM, Accenture, Deloitte, and all of the big firms. One key thing that differentiates us, which is where we have our own niche and our own league, is we offer fixed-cost with money back. We compete with the Big Five consulting firms and with some smaller ones. But we do not compare ourselves to them. We are running our own race, and we're making sure that we achieve our goals, which are distributed over the next one hundred years.

///

We have our own niche. We are the only consulting firm in the world that delivers fixed-cost solutions with a money-back guarantee.

•••

We are running our own race, and we're making sure that we achieve our goals, which are distributed over the next one hundred years.

///

HOW HAS THE CITY YOU'RE IN AFFECTED YOUR BUSINESS?

We have a global firm. Most of our employees, our consultants, work either from our headquarters here in Warrenville, Illinois, or in a big metropolitan area: New York City, Orlando, Zurich, Singapore, India, or Sydney. Being in Chicago, both when we were just getting started and now that we are established, has helped us tremendously because it is such a central location. Going to Los Angeles, New York, New Orleans, or even Europe is convenient and efficient. I can get to anyplace within the United States in a maximum of about four-and-a-half hours. If I need to go to Europe, it's seven or eight. In our profession, most of the work is done remotely, so as long as there is Internet availability, you're good wherever you live. But when we need to commute, being in a central place certainly helps.

WHAT WOULD YOU SAY TO YOUNG ENTREPRENEURS?

Being able to learn and to be open is critical. You need to keep that need for learning going strong. One of the people I look up to is Warren Buffett. Some people said he should have retired thirty years ago or more, but he's still strong. I believe that the key to his success and longevity is that he loves what he does and he keeps learning new things every day. Anyone who wants to be an entrepreneur should have a thirst for learning.

Anyone who wants to be an entrepreneur should have a thirst for learning.

Blake Fulton

MAG Trucks

BLAKE FULTON

CO-FOUNDER, MAG TRUCKS
KEARNEY, MISSOURI

Blake Fulton – MAG Trucks
Rank #81
3-Year % Growth: 2,932%
Revenue: $3.7 Million
Industry: Business Products & Services
# of Employees: 15
City/State: Kearney, MO

MAG Trucks is a Kearney, Missouri-based company that was founded by Blake Fulton and Brad Carlson in a University of Missouri dorm room. They founded MAG Trucks in 2007, when they were twenty-one-year-old undergraduates. The company has grown into an industry leader in truck delivery, fleet shipping, fleet management, and truck transportation. MAG Trucks offers a door-to-door relocation service for individual and commercial vehicles, as well as a refurbishing and outfitting service for step vans, straight trucks, and cutaways. MAG Trucks provides trucks to many industries—beverage, fire and emergency, linen and uniform, newspaper, and municipal—but its main clients are parcel delivery service companies.

Our growth rate has been approximately 3,000 percent, compounded over a three-year average rate. We had no goals in mind to start, but we did it. We definitely blew it out of the water. It's due to our dedicated focus. We had a clear strategy of what we wanted to do, and we didn't take on more than we should have. We've been lean with everything, which was kind of a product of the economy that we're in and of our general personalities.

We had a clear strategy of what we wanted to do, and we didn't take on more than we should have. We've been lean with everything.

I'd say the other part is we brought on great personnel. We also found a new niche market and we stuck to it, which goes back to that focus. It should not be understated that we also had a lot of fun. We tried to make everyone who worked with us focus on enjoying his or her job and having a fun time.

HOW DID YOU SET IT UP?

We're separated into three businesses, but we've brought two of those three in-house: the leasing company and the transport division. They had been kind of ancillary, but we brought them back in-house. We have some new things we're doing, including a body type. We're trying to develop some bodies and chassis for Federal Express and UPS. So that is keeping us busy. But our core business is still leasing and selling outfitted trucks to parcel delivery companies.

My best friend Brad and I started our business in college (actually, we started out of our dorm room). We had grown up around equipment, so we were always trying to do things here and there in that sector, trying to start something when we were young. This one took off.

We're five years into it now and in one year, we hope, we will be increasing revenue by about 50 percent. And it'll probably still be the same company. In four years, ultimately, we will have taken off and will have held on to a lot of the other ancillary stuff that we're doing, since it is gaining a foothold already. I imagine our business will have reached a plateau in four years, and our growth rate will have leveled off by then.

I imagine our business will have reached a plateau in four years, and our growth rate will have leveled off by then.

For us, reaching a plateau is not the worst thing, because we don't have any competitors who focus on our exact niche. Some people do similar work but they don't produce a similar product. They're just another solution. Technically, we don't have competitors.

DID YOUR LOCATION HELP?

We're in Kansas City, and we're happy to be here. When the economy went bad, it didn't affect us. Everything here is steady all the time. We don't have many lows or highs. They're doing this big push here, calling Kansas City "The City of Entrepreneurs," so that's helped out a lot. The city has been supportive. It's a great place to do business. And we're from here, so we love it for reasons other than its business opportunities.

The key to doing well in any business, no matter where you are, is fostering great relationships and keeping your word. Still, it's important to be able to establish a relationship and then, when you do something, to do *exactly* what you said you would. Once you've done that, you've got the client hooked forever. It's not so much trying to avoid doing a bad thing. It's making sure you do a good thing. The customers eat that up, as they should. We all like to patronize businesses that treat us well.

The key to doing well in any business, no matter where you are, is fostering great relationships and keeping your word.

•••

It's not so much trying to avoid doing a bad thing. It's making sure you do a good thing.

DOES AGE MATTER?

Brad and I are both still young, only twenty-five, but I think any entrepreneur should try to learn from failures early on, whether that means early in someone's working career or early in the life of his most recent business venture. The key is looking at other peoples' failures and learning from those. The idea is to learn from others' mistakes so that you do not commit your own, or at least none of any significance.

We always thought being young was going to be a big disadvantage, but then it turned out to be a big advantage. Many people seemed to want to share everything with us. We were never told, "No, we don't want to share this with you." Everyone always wanted to help. There were no disadvantages to being young entrepreneurs. Before we got started we believed our age might cause us some problems, but our own minds were what held us back. We had a slight fear of something that didn't exist. Looking back, if we had been older we probably would have been at a little bit of a disadvantage, because our spot in life would have been different and we would have had different expectations. However, actually, when we first started, we expected our business might do nothing or it might turn into something great. It came down to: "Do we like it, and is there an opportunity there?" The answer was yes.

Before we got started we believed our age might cause us some problems, but our own minds were what held us back.

•••

We were just trying to get something going. We never imagined it would get this big this quickly.

We were just trying to get something going. We never imagined it would get this big this quickly. I always wanted to run a growing company, but we didn't know how much we would grow. We didn't have any expectations about the size of our company or the rate of growth. In retrospect, when I look back at where we started and compare it to where we are today, honestly, I'm kind of surprised. I mean, we started this company in our dorm room at Mizzou [the University of Missouri].

I'm glad we did it. I think any college kid considering a business venture while he is still in college should take a hard look at his personality and determine what kind of person he is and what he wants out of his college years. Starting this business, as great as it is today, took a lot away from our college experience. Maybe our story is exciting to some people, and maybe to others it looks like we had our college experience stolen from us, or like we traded it for our business venture. It depends on your personality and what you want to do. However, I can tell you that when you get out of school and tell people you started your business out of your dorm room, it raises some eyebrows. People think it's cool. They love that story.

When you get out of school and tell people you started your business out of your dorm room, it raises some eyebrows. People think it's cool. They love that story.

WHAT DO YOU READ?

I read the *New York Times* every morning. I read *Business Insider* on my phone and I read this website called The Chive. It's actually not like reading; the site is just pictures. It's a pretty cool site. The book everyone should read is *The Tipping Point* by Malcolm Gladwell. That book taught me that you better go into something with a different perspective if you want to gain any insight. For instance, you can take mainstream media or whatever source you use for your research and go into it looking for something different than what you'd normally find. A different perspective. The book is all about perspectives. You apply those new perspectives, that new insight, to your business.

Not in a million years did I think I would be selling step vans to FedEx. I was into politics in college, so I always thought I would work in politics in some way or another. Then I realized I wanted to make money and not be broke. I thought I'd like to work for an investment firm or something like that. That's what I thought I'd end up doing. I'm glad I didn't. Come to think of it, I guess I changed my perspective early on and *The Tipping Point* confirmed what I already knew. That's one way of looking at it, at least.

I realized I wanted to make money and not be broke.

Bryan Mehr

M2 Displays Inc.

BRYAN MEHR

CO-FOUNDER, M2 DISPLAYS INC.
SANTA FE SPRINGS, CALIFORNIA

Bryan Mehr – M2 Displays Inc.
Rank #349
3-Year % Growth: 965%
Revenue: $4.2 Million
Industry: Business Products & Services
# of Employees: 12
City/State: Sante Fe Springs, CA

M2 Displays is a digital-wide and super-wide-format printing company that offers full-service commercial and wholesale visual graphics for banners, point of purchase displays, retail signage, and specialty printing. The company's founders saw a need for such services in 2007. Since then, the company has created an array of products, some of them never before attempted. M2 Displays tries to do whatever the customer asks; the company's executives believe this is where the growth of the printing industry lies. They predict their company will be on the forefront of that growth.

From 2008 to 2011, our growth rate was about 495 percent. Next year's rate will be much higher, since we're having a pretty good year. I would not say this year exceeded my expectations, because I have pretty high expectations of myself and of my company. Instead, I think that growth rate is probably right on target. I'm pleased with it.

WHAT IS RESPONSIBLE FOR YOUR TREMENDOUS GROWTH?

We are innovative. We do things and try things that a lot of people don't. We've printed on everything you can imagine, and there's a lot more out there. I look for unique materials and ideas because I know my printers are capable of printing on those things. That's part of why I started the company. I'm constantly trying to figure out new things [we can do at the company], and in doing that we've become known as people who will try just about anything. In fact, I got a call just now from a woman who heard we might be able to do a unique project for her. Being innovative is key for us.

We do things and try things that a lot of people don't.

•••

We always go over and above to meet our deadlines and our clients' deadlines. That seems pretty basic, but we do what we say we're going to do.

Service is also key. We always go over and above to meet our deadlines and our clients' deadlines. That seems pretty basic, but we do what we say we're going to do. That concept is summed up in the word *service*. Flexibility is another important thing for us. We have to be competitive in our industry, price-wise and in everything else. We have to be cautious of our overtime, so we hire employees and let them know up front we expect them to be flexible. If that means we need to switch them to a night shift, or if we need them to come in on the weekend, we want them to be flexible enough to do it.

Relationships are important. I had quite a few solid relationships prior to starting the company and those have grown. They've turned into referrals and many other contacts. We also work well with resellers. I would not say we're a trade shop, but one of our strategies has been to go to other companies that do similar work and have them sell what we do, which helps them increase their revenues on top of the customer base they already have. The hardest thing to do is get a good customer. If you already have a solid customer base, you need to offer that base another product and increase your revenues without having to go out and get a new customer. That strategy has worked well over the years.

///

The hardest thing to do is get a good customer.

///

I've been in the printing business a long time; I've seen the technology changing and getting better. The capabilities of doing out-of-the-box things, innovative things, were there, but I didn't see anybody willing to do them. The people I was working with who had the machines placed me in an awkward position. I worked closely with one company as a broker; the people there were willing to try things, but it was at a cost and it was on their timeframe. That didn't work.

The folks at the other company I worked with (as a broker) were not willing to try anything. They had a good price point, and they were fast, but they weren't willing to try different things. I thought, "I'm going to create a company in the middle that not only tries everything and anything, but that also offers a fair price point and does things fast." That's why I started my business; I felt there was a void, or a gap, in my particular industry.

Today my business is healthy. We're doing well from a financial standpoint. We have a good, solid customer base, and our clients are all doing well. We're poised to grow even faster and even more than we have already, which is great. One year from now, I think it's possible we could double where we are now. We've been growing so fast and so much that it's been a bit of a challenge keeping up. I don't know how that will factor into our ability to double within a year. It might be difficult to grow when we are working so hard to keep up with the business we already have.

It might be difficult to grow when we are working so hard to keep up with the business we already have.

We're a small company now. A year from now, we might cross the threshold to a medium company. Four years from now, we might be considered a major player in our sector of the printing business.

I think we are outrunning competitors because of the economy. We didn't plan on a recession when we started, but I think it has worked to our benefit. We're headed toward the big guys, the large print companies. There are a ton of small shops, and that's not where we want to be. That's not where our future is. The recession affected many of the big shops badly. In fact, a lot of them closed down. They could not stay above water. That allowed us to purchase equipment cheaply. While we were on an upswing, many of our competitors were on a downswing or closing down altogether. There's still a ton of work out there. When one big company closes down, where does that work go? Well, it found its way to us because we were in the right place at the right time.

***

There's still a ton of work out there. When one big company closes down, where does that work go?

***

We've moved three times now. We started in one city, moved to another, and then moved to Santa Fe Springs, California. I don't think the city helps or hurts us that much. Strategically, we're close to Los Angeles, between L.A. and Orange County, and there's a ton of business here. But we only moved here because our sister company is right around the corner. The other reason was we needed more space and this was a good place to get that space for a low cost.

We are on the West Coast, and I think most big printing jobs and contracts go to companies on the East Coast or in the Midwest, where the biggest printing companies are. There is a need on the West Coast, and we're here to fill that need. In fact, Walmart just started sending a ton of work out here to California. We didn't get a contract with them, but we're getting a lot of work from a printer that did.

SO, GENERALLY SPEAKING, THE WEST COAST IS A FACTOR BUT YOUR SPECIFIC TOWN IS NOT?

I think so. When I make presentations to potential clients, I say, "I know you have distribution out here and you're doing all of your printing back there. We can save you 'this much' on shipping if you do some of your printing out here." It's a selling point and I think it's a valid one.

HOW DO YOU SUCCEED IN THE PRINTING BUSINESS WHEN THERE IS SO MUCH COMPETITION?

You have to do what you say you're going to do. Meet deadlines. Do it better than the other guys, basically. There's so much work out there. Continuing to do it better than others is becoming one of my biggest challenges. That's what got me here, but the more we grow and the faster we grow, it becomes more and more challenging to meet those deadlines all the time. But it's key, absolutely key, to our future.

Cash flow is an important concept for any entrepreneur. When I first started the company, my philosophy was sell, sell, sell. I'm good at it, and I thought as long as I sell, as long as I keep bringing work in, we're going to do well. However, about two years into the business, I thought, "I can't pay my bills. I'm selling tons of work. What is going on?" As you grow your business, you're constantly trying to pay your vendors, while you're waiting for money to come in from your clients. The faster you grow, it seems, the harder it is to catch up. I think getting a handle on your cash flow early on is a big lesson to learn. If I had it to do over, I would pay more attention to that.

Cash flow is an important concept for any entrepreneur.

•••

Getting a handle on your cash flow early on is a big lesson to learn.

WHAT'S YOUR READING ROUTINE?

I read the Bible in the morning. I read Proverbs during the day, and I have a little book here by John Mason titled *An Enemy Called Average*. It's a Biblical book; it's made up of little nuggets you read every day to keep yourself motivated and on the right track. That's my favorite book, by the way: the Bible.

I also read *Inc.* magazine. I read *Bass Company*, I love *Wired* magazine, and I read quite a bit of news. There are readers on my tablet that I read: technical stuff, technology, electronics, and things like that. I'm always trying to study up on the latest and greatest.

If I ever wrote a book on my own, it would be about common sense. I think about common sense all the time. Honestly, I think that's one of the biggest things lacking in our society. I feel like some people have it and some people don't, and I don't know why.

Gerard Ferro

Free For All Inc.

GERARD FERRO

FOUNDER AND CEO, FREE FOR ALL INC.
PHILADELPHIA, PENNSYLVANIA

Gerard Ferro – Free For All Inc.
Rank #151
3-Year % Growth: 1,871%
Revenue: $2.5 Million
Industry: Health
# of Employees: 17
City/State: Mt. Laurel, NJ

Free for All Inc. designs, develops, and administers discount medical prescription programs for consumers with limited or no access to typical health insurance plans. Free For All Inc. programs are not technically insurance plans; instead, they are designed to be the "next best thing." The company relies on a staff of marketing, healthcare, and technology professionals to find solutions to common problems that scores of Americans face every day: getting affordable prescriptions.

Our percentage over three years is 907 percent. We actually exceeded our projections. We've got a board, we're pretty meticulous, and I try to under-promise and over-deliver. It's how we operate, and our board is always extremely happy. We've actually had a tremendous run and we're still growing.

HOW ARE YOU DOING IT?

First and foremost, it's my team. I think the economy plays a huge role. I guess the next component is education and awareness. Once people understand what our product is and does, they continue to use it and they spread the word. So, we grow organically by about 11 percent a month. Awards and media also help. Awards attract attention and that generates press about what we do.

///

We grow organically by about 11 percent a month.

///

HOW HAS YOUR TEAM HELPED YOU GROW?

We all have our areas of expertise, and we all have our strengths and weaknesses. My team and I have an unbelievable balance. No matter what it is, we hit the ground running. We've basically been doing a different version of the same thing through three companies and three different areas of health care. We have been together for a long time. We have a core team, and it's easy to impose the team's culture on the rest of the company.

It makes life a lot easier when everyone is focused and knows what the job is. We sit down for a weekly executive meeting. Once a month, we break bread formally, at a dinner. We're tuned in to one another. My IT executive always brings his three guys, who are my main guys, with him. My VP of customer service always brings her top two with her. So, we build. We have a good solid core, and when you have that, it's easy to grow.

My team and I have an unbelievable balance. No matter what it is, we hit the ground running.

•••

We sit down for a weekly executive meeting. Once a month, we break bread formally, at a dinner. We're tuned in to one another.

HOW IS WHAT YOU'RE DOING DIFFERENT THAN WHAT YOUR COMPETITORS ARE DOING?

What we do right now is hand out a free prescription drug card that saves people a tremendous amount of money whether they have insurance or not—but particularly if they do. People who have a generic co-pay of $10 or higher are probably paying more than the cash price for their medications.

With the economy being what it is, every dollar counts. In the case of people taking multiple medications on a maintenance basis, you can save them money. Sometimes we get testimonials, people saying, "You saved me $600," "You saved me $300," "You saved me $150," or "You saved me $49." Year-to-date we've saved customers a total of $65 million. It's a tremendous number if you think about it, and this is only our fourth year.

To put it into perspective, in 2010 companies processed 3.9 billion prescriptions. Of those, 94 percent were processed by one of three publicly traded companies: CVS Caremark, Express Scripts, and Medco. Now, it's two. Express Scripts just bought Medco for… are you sitting down? $29 billion.

In 2010, the gross revenue per prescription for CVS Caremark was the most profitable gross overcharge of the trade at $75 per prescription. Medco and Express Scripts overcharged $68 and $69 and change, respectively. The next number is going to rock you: 92 percent of all those prescriptions were generic medications. These companies are making that kind of gross revenue per prescription for generic medications, and they bill people for myriad practices. One is charging the co-pay, let alone giving a customer the real discount, when the cash price is less. If I can provide "Product A" for $7.20 instead of $15, why can't Medco do the same? Medco's got a much better discount than I do.

Year-to-date we've saved customers a total of $65 million.

•••

If I can provide "Product A" for $7.20 instead of $15, why can't Medco do the same? Medco's got a much better discount than I do.

WHY CAN'T THEY DO THE SAME THING FOR THE CUSTOMER AND SELL IT FOR $5?

I started this business to help others and to attack a huge problem while I'm doing it. It's a fair day's work and a fair day's pay model. I don't charge a percentage of the savings, so if I save somebody a huge amount, I win big. It's a static $2.50, and I only collect it when I win. I win eight out of ten times. However, suppose the cash price is both better than my price and better than a person's insurance co-pay, but my discount is still not as good as the cash price. My company imposes no disadvantage on that person. In other words, there is no penalty and no way to get caught financially. We have no tricks up our sleeve. That person will get that cash price and it will cost me 12 cents—6 cents comes to me and 6 cents goes toward the cash price.

I started this business to help others and to attack a huge problem while I'm doing it. It's a fair day's work and a fair day's pay model.

•••

I only collect it when I win. I win eight out of ten times.

This is not like the Pharmaceutical Benefit Managers' model, which benefits PBMs only; they truly grab every nickel, dime, and quarter they can, everywhere they can. They can't afford to operate at our level of efficiency. For us, that's where technology comes in. We don't need a $75 gross receipt to operate our organization. We operate on $2.50.

It's a significant difference, and we provide the same material services. The same services.

WHERE IS YOUR BUSINESS GOING?

At this point, we are working toward a major stock buyback of the company. That's already been executed, agreed upon, and put in place. We officially bought back our first round of stock this month. In twelve months, we're going to buy another $1.1 million worth of shares, which is essentially the remaining stock, outside of stock owned by some insiders, friends, and family. We'll be completely debt-free at that point.

While we're doing that, we're also executing an expansion in all of our departments: marketing, customer service, and technology. Hiring developers is going to increase our ability to get into certain markets. We're moving heavily into the e-prescribing space. There is a lot of technology out there, bulletin board-type stuff, which we're looking to develop. We're also looking to develop phone apps that will make it easier to use our free products.

Our competitors can't afford to compete with us. The industry we're in is the only one that can dial its profit. Say a company's earning target, hypothetically, is $76.50. The number's at $75.50, and they need an extra buck to hit their earnings numbers, so their stock keeps going, and all they need to do is take a look at the utilization. Suppose they have 35 million Lipitor prescriptions getting refilled today and 2 million of something else. All they have to do is tweak the numbers. Instead of $1.99, they raise it to $2.13. They can pick up their dollar shortfall in 10 seconds. This is the only industry that can do that. The only industry.

I don't need to dial anything in. I have a flat $2.50 fee. Overall, there's $3.9 billion. How much of that is up for grabs in the insurance market? That doesn't even count the 52 million people without health insurance in the United States, or the 45-plus million undocumented citizens in this country. We have an opportunity to go out and take a huge piece of this market at a nominal fee of $2.50, while I'm helping consumers immensely. The only ones who lose in this situation are the over-compensated PBMs. That's the beauty of it. The pharmacy makes more money. The consumers, our members, save up to 50 percent or more of their co-pays on generics probably eight out of ten times.

The industry we're in is the only one that can dial its profit.

•••

We have an opportunity to go out and take a huge piece of this market.

DOES IT MATTER WHERE YOU ARE?

Being in Philadelphia as long as I have, I have a lot of tremendous contacts. It certainly helps when you are launching a new business to get in doors that otherwise might be a little more difficult. I think my reputation in the community is such that I can get into places more easily than I could in, let's say, Chicago. I didn't choose Philadelphia. It chose me. I never left; I just made it work. I grew up in the city, and I didn't know anything but the city.

WHAT DO YOU READ?

I get news and market feeds on my iPhone. In the morning I usually deal with overnight e-mails first. I subscribe to about eight different business magazines. During the week I read different business magazines, and on the weekends I read or listen to books. I download a lot of books on audio. I'm getting older, so my eyes are usually tired by the end of the week from reading all of the e-mails and text messages. I think *The Tipping Point* by Malcolm Gladwell is a book everyone should read.

ANY ADVICE FOR NEW ENTREPRENEURS?

When you get knocked down, and you surely will, get back up quickly.

When you get knocked down, and you surely will, get back up quickly.

Jeremy Larson

Deluxe Marketing Inc.

JEREMY LARSON

CHAIRMAN AND CEO, DELUXE MARKETING INC.
SAN JOSE, CALIFORNIA

Jeremy Larson – Deluxe Marketing Inc.
Rank #227
3-Year % Growth: 1,410%
Revenue: $9.1 Million
Industry: Advertising & Marketing
# of Employees: 12
City/State: Las Vegas, NV

Deluxe Marketing Inc. (DMI) provides professional marketing and contracting services to the telecommunications, cable, and retail industries for companies such as Comcast Cable, Adelphia, Time Warner Cable, Target Stores, Walmart, Sam's Club, Kohl's, Chase, Bloomingdales, and Lowe's. Specifically, DMI provides staffing for door-to-door sales, business-to-business sales, retail kiosks, and special event marketing. DMI has more than 400 direct sales representatives and technicians in fifteen major markets; its corporate staff has more than 30 years of experience in face-to-face marketing and presentations.

Over the last three years, our growth rate was 1,410 percent. We ranked number 227 on the *Inc.* 500 list. In the three years prior, we actually doubled those numbers. We had a growth rate of 2,822 percent, and we were 85 on the *Inc.* 500 list for 2010.

DID THAT SURPRISE YOU?

Yes. Obviously, there is a point where you see it coming, and you know the iron's hot and it's time to strike. Looking back, we definitely exceeded expectations. Do I expect to grow year after year? Of course I do, but to have achieved that level of growth at that rate definitely was not something we expected.

///

Do I expect to grow year after year? Of course I do.

•••

The top five things responsible for our growth start with number one: passion.

///

HOW DID YOU DO IT?

The top five things responsible for our growth start with number one: passion. I think you've got to have a proper mindset to build a company that's going to grow. You've got to have a burning passion and wake up every morning wanting to go to work on that business. Number two would be mission. For us, it was important to have a mission— something to stand up for or to fight for. Number three is vision. We look at how things are and at how we want them to be, and then we go to work on that gap in the middle.

Number four is definitely strategy. You have a system, or plan, and then you have to be able to execute that plan or fall back, review it, and make any needed alterations. Number five, which might sound funny, is guts. Having the heart to stand by your decisions and being fearless when considering what other people think is essential. I believe going around trying to make everybody happy is a real recipe for disaster.

I believe going around trying to make everybody happy is a real recipe for disaster.

Passion, mission, and vision have been part of our thinking all along. When I was younger, I drove myself, and the organization, through pure passion. I don't think I fully appreciated how valuable it was to have strategy and systems in place. I do now. That was a new idea for me. So was the concept of having guts. I didn't fully understand how important that was. Again, when I talk about guts, I'm talking about sticking to your mission and your plan. When I was younger, sometimes I tried to make everybody happy, but that's impossible. For me, strategy and guts were things I picked up along the way.

HOW DID YOU GET INTO YOUR BUSINESS?

I started the business out of pure passion. I knew what I wanted to do, I knew how I wanted to do it, and I had a burning passion for that. I felt what we were going to do, what we were going to bring to the table, was a missing piece in our industry. In my mind, we were solving a problem. We were bringing something to the industry that wasn't exactly there before. That was the "why." The "how" resulted from a major drive to not give up, but to be resourceful and adaptable. The game plan you have in place from the start may not be the one you end up following. Being adaptable, tapping into resources, and being creative, was the big "how" for us.

///

The game plan you have in place from the start may not be the one you end up following.

///

My burning desire and passion was to be part of an organization that focused on personal development and allowed people to have a positive influence on the team. I was drawn to the idea of building a real team atmosphere and creating a platform from which somebody could start at the back of the line and make it all the way up to the front with a lot of hard work and discipline. We didn't see that in the direct sales industry. Specifically, we didn't see that in the telecommunications industry. We didn't see companies operating with that philosophy. I thought, "Gosh, wouldn't it be great if this existed? I'm going to do this."

Our industry is like most industries right now—there's a lot of change happening. We look different today than how we looked two or three years ago. We are much more efficient than we've been in the past. We've put a major focus on being efficient from all angles and making sure the energy, money, and time is being invested most efficiently in order to get the return we desire. In a year I expect us to be much more of a lean machine than we've been in the past. Yet I expect us to keep growing. Four years from now, I think we'll still focus on efficiency, but who's to say? Things change often and they change fast.

I feel we have been able to achieve and outrun our competitors through preparation. I heard a friend and mentor say, "You can beat anybody and anything if you are willing to work harder, prepare harder, and practice more than your opponent." Taking that approach—focusing on the effort and the preparation to be successful, launch into a new market, open up a new office, and double the size of the company—has been a key factor for us in outrunning our competitors.

I heard a friend and mentor say, "You can beat anybody and anything if you are willing to work harder, prepare harder, and practice more than your opponent."

DOES BEING IN THE MIDDLE OF THE TECH WORLD AFFECT YOUR BUSINESS?

One of our main offices is in San Jose, California, and the city hasn't had too much of an effect on our business. The first city we started working in was the first market we did business with: Tucson, Arizona. That was a no-brainer. We went out there temporarily to get started. Now we have over twenty-five offices in twenty-five different cities. San Jose happens to be where I live. It's a great city for entrepreneurs. It has movement; it has momentum. There's a lot going on here. For us it hasn't been much of a factor, but for entrepreneurs in general, I think it's a great place to be.

The key to being successful is being adaptable. In our industry things change daily. Being adaptable to those changes, focusing on the positive and the good that can come out of them, has been key to our success. If you get caught up in an old way of thinking, you'll be left behind.

The key to being successful is being adaptable.

•••

There have been situations in which we could have cut a corner and possibly gained something from it, but we always stuck to integrity.

The most important lesson an entrepreneur could learn, in my opinion, is to never sacrifice integrity for growth. That's something we take a lot of pride in. We've always walked that straight line. There have been situations in which we could have cut a corner and possibly gained something from it, but we always stuck to integrity and never sacrificed that for growth. That's helped us build our reputation. It's helped us keep clients longer than any of our competitors. It's helped us build relationships and partnerships, and gain testimonials and referrals. I cannot express how important it is, especially when you are starting out, to stick to integrity and make that a core value in your business.

I'm a big reader: I do thirty minutes every morning. I call it "thirty to thrive." It's a great way to start the day, spending those first thirty minutes reading. I read books focused on personal development, business, marketing, and leadership. I'm interested in anything in the business genre.

The book that changed my life when I was younger was *Think and Grow Rich* by Napoleon Hill. It opened my eyes to a lot of opportunity, possibilities, and ways to think. It had a huge influence on the path I took. If I were to write a book, I would like it to be about overcoming adversity as an entrepreneur. We've shown a level of growth of more than $10 million in revenue over the last two years, and we're having a great year right now, so I think I would be qualified to write that book. I wouldn't try to speak on something I hadn't been through myself.

John Kellogg

Square Peg Packaging

JOHN KELLOGG

PRESIDENT, SQUARE PEG PACKAGING AND PRINTING
SAN DIEGO, CALIFORNIA

John Kellogg – Square Peg Packaging
Rank #34
3-Year % Growth: 5,986%
Revenue: $7.4 Million
Industry: Business Products & Services
# of Employees: 8
City/State: Poway, CA

Square Peg started with a simple idea. It's amazing that the idea is not more widespread across the two industries Square Peg represents. The company provides both printing and packaging services—many clients use two separate vendors for these services—and they deliver fast. "Fast" is part of their philosophy: get the job done right away and get it done right. By putting both operations under one roof, Square Peg saves its customers money, and that, of course, results in more customers. The company also offers aggressive design and printing services that many other printers shy away from.

Square Peg creates point-of-purchase displays and direct-mail advertising materials, among many others.

I don't have our current percentage handy, but I think last time we were on the *Inc.* 500 list it was somewhere around 6,000 percent, or some ridiculous amount. This year, believe it or not, it pretty much met our expectations.

HOW SO?

We're a little aggressive in our philosophy when it comes to growth, but yes, it's pretty much in line. Maybe it's slightly above what we had planned for the company over our first three or four years. The funny part is, we still feel like it's nowhere near where we want to be. We're just never satisfied, it seems. We celebrate for a brief moment, and then we put our heads back down and start pushing again to achieve the next thing.

The funny part is, we still feel like it's nowhere near where we want to be.

•••

We have a culture, an expectation, of growing no matter what. No excuses.

HOW DO YOU DO IT?

It's pretty clearly defined with us. First, we foster a culture of growth. We are a growth company and always will be. We have a culture, an expectation, of growing no matter what. No excuses. Second, we have true diversification. We truly believe that if you're not clearly different than others, you're just playing a price game. We differentiate ourselves from others in our marketplace. Third, we hire only passionate and dedicated people. Everybody who works here lives and breathes our mission. Our people have gotten us to where we are, period.

Fourth, our conservative financial management is also key. We believe in aggressive growth but conservative financial management. We believe in extremely minimal debt, which keeps us focused on growth, not servicing a debt-ridden company. Fifth—and this probably should have been first— I've got the most understanding and wonderful wife and kids a guy could ever have. This place would have tanked in the first year if they hadn't been so supportive, because working seven days a week, 14 hours a day, for the first few years takes a lot of understanding from an entrepreneur's family. I have two young kids who are seven and eleven, and my wife and I have been married for nineteen years. Boy, I tell you: that should have been number one instead of number five. A lot of things will change in our business, from products and services to people and buildings. But these five things—they are just who we are.

WHY DID YOU START THIS SPECIFIC COMPANY?

I have twenty years of experience in our product lines and in printing and packaging. But the real reason we started the company is we saw a niche in the market. It goes back to that differentiation; historically, printing and packaging have come from two separate suppliers. They seem similar, but they are extremely different in terms of how they operate in those specific businesses. Typically, clients had a printing supplier and a packaging supplier. We saw a niche and said, "What if we could put those two things together, with true expertise, and bring one service to the market so customers could increase their brand consistency?"

Their printing would actually match their packaging because it would all come from one supplier. They could reduce vendors. They could save money. We had never seen that done before. That was the primary reason we started the company. The second reason was a timing issue. We started on Oct. 1, 2007. We saw the economic crisis, since it had started at that point. We were right at the crux of it. We knew it was going to be worse than everybody thought. Everybody thought we were nuts for starting a company in 2007, but we thought the opposite. We thought it was an awesome time to start a company. After all, in a crisis, what are companies looking for? They're looking for cost savings. They're looking for a reduction in the capital needed to run their businesses. In 2007, we knew lending was going to dry up. Companies would try to do more with less because they were laying people off and cutting in other areas.

We thought it was the perfect time to start a young, aggressive, non-debt-ridden company with a new business model pulling two industries together. We thought it was the perfect time to help our customers navigate the recession. And, knock on wood, I think we were right. We have our company purpose and central beliefs. Our purpose has to do with enhancing our customers' competitiveness and success. We thought, in an economic crisis, we were creating a great way to do that: consolidating services and offering them to companies who were making cuts of their own.

Everybody thought we were nuts for starting a company in 2007, but we thought the opposite.

•••

We thought it was the perfect time to help our customers navigate the recession. And, knock on wood, I think we were right.

Despite how well we've done, we feel as though we've just begun. We have our five-year anniversary coming up at the end of this year, and it feels as though we've just scratched the surface. Today it looks like we're just starting to hit our stride. We're profitable, growing, and enthusiastic. That's a snapshot of what our business looks like today. In a year, we will have added an entirely new product category. Now we have printing, packaging, and a services division, and we'll add a fourth within the next year. That's going to, again, add a whole other industry to what we can do.

We'll have our first geographic expansion done in the next year, our first out-of-state location, and that's exciting. In four years, I think it's going to be more of the same. We'll have four or five locations at that point. But we are also going to invest in our business services side. Four years out, that's going to be a huge part of our company.

HOW IS YOUR BUSINESS OUTRUNNING YOUR COMPETITORS?

I'd love to say a million reasons, but it boils down to speed and passion. On a daily basis, we run faster than anybody. We have a "we don't sleep 'til it's done" attitude. Our competitors have a hard time keeping up with our speed, and that is a credit to our people. Strategically, in a larger context, we're winning by moving the goalposts as often as we can. What that means is we are adding new products and new services. Right about the time the competition is trying to catch up with our daily speed and sprint, we like to leapfrog over them. By the time they're ready to try and catch up with our speed and what we're currently doing, we announce a whole new category and put them back on their heels again.

Strategically, in a larger context, we're winning by moving the goalposts as often as we can.

WHAT DO MEAN BY YOUR "SPEED"? DOES THAT REFER TO OUTPUT OR TO COMING UP WITH NEW PRODUCTS AND IDEAS?

It's both. We're in a fast-paced business. Our customers can't put their product out the door without our product because our product, the packaging, is the thing they wrap their product in. Our printing tends to be exceptionally fast. We execute jobs faster than our competition does. Whether it is just a simple, direct-mail piece that someone wants us to print and drop in the mail or a whole Costco pallet display for an electronics company, we can bring the product to market and execute on a daily basis faster than anyone else. Our speed has less to do with product development and more to do with execution on a job-by-job basis.

Our speed has less to do with product development and more to do with execution on a job-by-job basis.

ANY SPECIFIC REASONS YOU ARE BASED IN SAN DIEGO?

I was born and raised in San Diego, and I love this place. I love the town; I love the feel. The weather's not bad in San Diego, either. It's a big city and it's competitive, although not as much as a Chicago or a Los Angeles. San Diego seemed like the perfect place to start. Then we moved into major markets as we expanded. I have a soft spot for San Diego.

Every time I hire a new employee and add to the prosperity of San Diego, I get a kick out of it. I like to help the city.

People are the key to success. We call our team members "Square Peggers" after Square Peg, the name of the company. I can't underline enough how much our employees have worked and sacrificed to get the company where it is. It's almost a balancing act, because they are so passionate and they work so hard. I want them to enjoy that, but sometimes I'm afraid they will work themselves too hard and get burned out or start to struggle. I've got to admit, I haven't always done a great job of knowing where that line is, but I've continued to work on making sure we don't get people to the point where they've burned out.

I have to give credit to John Rubey and Josh Wright. They both sell for the company, but they've also become partners in the business. Without these two guys, the company would not be what it is. They've humbled me and pushed me to be a better leader because they are so aggressive and so good at what they do. It's important to me to mention them by name and call them out specifically, but, in general, people have been key to our success. A lot of people are doing printing, and a lot of people are doing packaging. We're not building patented products here. We have to be better, smarter, and faster than the rest in order to win, and you can only do that through your people.

A good lesson for an entrepreneur to learn is this: you've got to watch your debt. I'm old school when it comes to debt. I see a lot of companies starting out. The first thing they do is borrow a bunch of money, and then all they do is spend their time servicing their debt instead of growing their sales. Minimize your debt at all costs.

I've continued to work on making sure we don't get people to the point where they've burned out.

•••

A lot of people are doing printing, and a lot of people are doing packaging. We're not building patented products here.

•••

A good lesson for an entrepreneur to learn is this: you've got to watch your debt.

I love to read books. Everybody in business should read *Built to Last* by James Collins. Fantastic book. I've read it probably ten times, cover-to-cover, in my career. My copy is outlined, noted, and beaten up like you wouldn't believe.

Jon Spencer

Landmark Retail Corp.

JON SPENCER

PRESIDENT, LANDMARK RETAIL CORP.

LITTLE FALLS, NEW JERSEY

Jon Spencer – Landmark Retail Corp.

Rank #161

3-Year % Growth: 1,825%

Revenue: $2.7 Million

Industry: Construction

# of Employees: 8

City/State: Little Falls, NJ

Landmark Retail Corp. is a retail construction and maintenance company founded in 2009, at the height of the most recent American recession. Tony Pizza had been let go from his job in the construction industry, and Jon Spencer, another construction and facilities-industry veteran, was looking to do something new. They teamed up and formed Landmark, which builds retail space for some of the world's top fashion designers, including Hermès of Paris, Zara, Juicy Couture, Kate Spade, Lucky Brand Jeans, Diesel USA, and ZILLY.

Our growth was 1,825 percent. I wouldn't say it exceeded our expectations. We knew we were going to have rapid growth from the time we opened our doors. We're pleased with it, and we hope to continue that rate as long as we possibly can. I know at some point that rate is going to diminish.

HOW WERE YOU ABLE TO HAVE SUCH A STRONG START?

The main thing is dedication. We had a commitment to what we were doing and wanted to do anything we could to make that work. In addition, we sacrificed. The hours you put in once you make that commitment are just astonishing. We were working 110-hour weeks, literally. I think one year I worked 363 days. It comes with a price, but we were willing to make that sacrifice.

Outside of that, it takes superior communication with our clients. Even though we are a construction company, most of what we do and why we get the kind of work we do is because of information flow. We make a big effort to keep our customers in the loop as to what's going on with their projects at any time: day, night, and around the clock, seven days a week. That communication sets us apart.

We were working 110-hour weeks, literally. I think one year I worked 363 days.

•••

It's no phony car salesmanship for us. It's personal. In other words, we've got friendships with our customers—each and every one of them.

Aside from that, my business partner Tony Pizza and I have a personal relationship with our customers. It's no phony car salesmanship for us. It's personal. In other words, we've got friendships with our customers—each and every one of them. That helps us develop.

I wouldn't say any of these are new ideas. It's just a common-sense method of doing business. Most entrepreneurs are going to have the wherewithal to perform these things. They know they're going to have to dedicate themselves. They know they're going to have to make a tremendous sacrifice.

HOW DID YOU GET INTO THIS BUSINESS?

When I was seventeen years old, I sat down, and in 15 minutes I wrote out a life plan. I said to myself, "From this point forward, I'm going to start with this, and then I'm going to do this, then I'm going to do this, and then I'm going to do this." Somewhere on that life plan was the idea to "start a national construction company." In 2007, when we were in the midst of a pretty severe recession, my close friend and former co-worker Tony Pizza got laid off. He and I spoke. We got together and said, "Let's do this." Considering his knowledge of construction and my business background, we decided it was the right time. It blended together perfectly. As of today, our business is continuing to grow at the same rate as it did for the last three years. We expect to make the *Inc.* 500 list again. That's how things look now.

///

When I was seventeen years old, I sat down, and in 15 minutes I wrote out a life plan.

///

One year down the road, we want to continue our growth by adding clients. Our client base increases by about 30 percent every year, and that is pivotal to our growth. Four years down the road, we have two things to consider. First, since we started the company three years ago, we've moved locations three times because we've continually outgrown our offices. What we're looking to do now is acquire a building that's large enough to support our growth for the next four years, as we continue to add staff. Second, four years from now we want to add offices on the West Coast, in the Southeast, and in the Chicago area, so we cover the central region.

HOW IS YOUR BUSINESS DIFFERENT FROM OTHER NATIONAL CONSTRUCTION COMPANIES?

What sets us apart is having different departments. A lot of national construction companies do one thing. They do, say, maintenance for retail stores around the country. Others do alterations. Others do new store construction. They'll do pretty much one of those things, and that's their concentration. We do all three. We have a maintenance division. If anything breaks in the store, or fails, we get calls and dispatch people, 24 hours a day, around the country. We do renovations; when a company wants to spruce up an existing store, we take care of that. We also do new store construction. I think that's one thing that helps us to stay ahead of our competition: our diversity of services.

We are in Little Falls, New Jersey. Little Falls doesn't affect our business one bit. We don't do any business anywhere near it. But our proximity to Manhattan does help us in that many of our clients, the people we build or service retail stores for, are in the fashion industry, and many of them have their headquarters in Manhattan. We're able to get there in an hour or half an hour. We can easily be in and out of Manhattan for "press-the-flesh" meetings, and that helps. But it's not completely necessary. Little Falls is just where we're from. I could operate this business from Alaska.

That's one thing that helps us to stay ahead of our competition: our diversity of services.

•••

I could operate this business from Alaska.

REGARDLESS OF YOUR LOCATION, WHAT IS ONE THING THAT WOULD NOT CHANGE NO MATTER WHERE YOU WERE BASED?

Customer service. I know that sounds clichéd, but our clients know that. This is an extension of an earlier idea, but our clients know that on any given day they can call me, 24 hours a day. They can call my partner 24 hours a day. Cell phones, home phones, weekends, Sundays—we are always available. It's not as though we've grown to a point at which I pass off my clients who have helped us grow and say, "Okay, here's the person who is going to be your account manager. I'm going to step out of it because I'm too important now."

We maintain those personal relationships. I think that's a big part of our success, as is realizing the company you built is an extension of yourself. They are not to be separated. You need to be available for your customers at all times. It doesn't matter who they are. If it's your smallest customer or your largest customer calling, it doesn't matter; if that phone rings, you answer it. On top of that, it's always good to be honest, straightforward, and personable. By extending yourself and making yourself available, you develop close relationships with your customers.

It's not as though we've grown to a point at which I pass off my clients who have helped us grow and say, "Okay, here's the person who is going to be your account manager. I'm going to step out of it because I'm too important now."

•••

If it's your smallest customer or your largest customer calling, it doesn't matter; if that phone rings, you answer it.

WHAT IS YOUR READING ROUTINE?

My business partner Tony reads the paper every day. For me, it's just regular book reading every single night before I go to bed, without exception. And my weekend *New York Times*.

That's pretty much it. The one book I always go back to is the first book I read that had any kind of business self-help, organizational focus. It's a simple book that I re-read every single year. It's called *How to Get Control of Your Time and Your Life*, and it's by Alan Lakein. It's a simple, short book, maybe one hundred pages. I always go back to it because it helps me keep my head screwed on straight.

If I were ever to write a book of my own, it would be about persistence, perseverance, and just getting out and doing things without any preconceived notions of limitations. If you think you can't do it, you damn well can't.

We started this company from scratch four years ago. I started with one $250 job. It went from there. If you know what you're doing and you believe in it, there are no limitations. There's nothing you can't do. The preconceived notions need to be dismissed. If you want to do it, do it.

If you know what you're doing and you believe in it, there are no limitations.

Jud "Bo" Clift

ASE Direct, Inc.

JUD "BO" CLIFT

CEO, ASE DIRECT, INC.

FRANKLIN, TENNESSEE

Jud "Bo" Clift – ASE Direct, Inc.

Rank #291

3-Year % Growth: 1,124%

Revenue: $4 Million

Industry: Government Services

# of Employees: 13

City/State: Franklin, TN

ASE Direct specializes in Internet technology supplies, hardware, and office supplies, aiding the daily operations of large private corporations, federal government offices, and data centers across the world. ASE Direct's core product line consists of a full complement of IT supplies, equipment, and data storage media devices from seventy leading manufacturers. The company's founder is Bo Clift, a service-disabled veteran and a graduate of the United States Military Academy at West Point, where he played wide receiver for the Cadets from 1997 to 2000.

Last year we were number 291 on the *Inc.* 500 list with 1,124 percent growth over the last three years. The growth rate did not exceed our expectations because we were confident we could provide our clients with a total turnkey, best-value proposition that we thought the competition was not providing. In addition to that [providing what the competition doesn't], to be successful, you need great, loyal employees; integrated technology and systems; innovative market strategy to bring in new products; and you need to listen. None of these are new ideas or techniques, but we took them and stayed focused, at the core, and then we repeated the ideas over and over.

HOW DID YOU START YOUR BUSINESS?

I started the business from a kitchen counter. I focused the business on revenue, and then I personally negotiated with vendors who had a purchase order in hand and who had credit cards. So I did not need big capital financing—just a customer with a credit card and a purchase order. I had no formal office, either. I negotiated with vendors at my kitchen table. There was an urgent market need for the product and service we could bring. The competition just wasn't bringing it. They either wouldn't or couldn't. But we could.

I started the business from a kitchen counter.

•••

I negotiated with vendors at my kitchen table.

WHY THIS BUSINESS?

We deal with anything underneath the office supply and technology umbrella, and those are two types of products that every viable business needs. It's consumable and for us it provides repeat, recurring revenue. Today, we are experiencing exponential growth. We acquire new customers on a daily basis. After one year, we've got a contract on a new 12,000-square-foot building, and we plan to double our employees. In four years…dream big, be big. Think small, be small. In four years, I predict we will continue to beat our forecasts, quarter after quarter, and have to revise our budgets every quarter, which is a great thing. If you can actually pinpoint where you're going to be in four years, either you're not growing enough or you've got such a maintained business that it's stagnant. So when I think of four years from now, I just think: dream big, be big.

We deal with anything underneath the office supply and technology umbrella, and those are two types of products that every viable business needs.

•••

If you can actually pinpoint where you're going to be in four years, either you're not growing enough or you've got such a maintained business that it's stagnant.

We outrun our competitors by making real-time business decisions without all of the corporate American bureaucracy and lack of decision making that holds back so many other companies. When a market need comes up, or an enterprise-type client opportunity comes up, we make decisions right then and there. We can turn like a jet ski. The big box stores—Computer Discount Warehouse, Dell, Office Depot, and Staples—turn like a Carnival cruise ship. When we make a decision, we can cut at a 90-degree angle. And by the time we've made that decision, we've made four other decisions that have put us four steps in front of our competitors.

We can turn like a jet ski. The big box stores—Computer Discount Warehouse, Dell, Office Depot, and Staples—turn like a Carnival cruise ship.

We are an international business, so our city hasn't positively or negatively impacted the company much. One positive has been the great employee talent pool Nashville has. We have benefited from that, and we have had some great employees who have been loyal to us. I actually grew up here, in the area; this is where I've always lived, and I love it. I've traveled a lot and I didn't want the business to dictate where I was going. I dictated where the business was going.

WHAT'S THE KEY TO BEING SUCCESSFUL IN YOUR INDUSTRY?

Always be closing (ABC). It might be a cliché in the sense that whatever your product, widget, service, or technology is, if you're not selling a lot of it, and you're not always closing new business, you're getting beat. To beat the competition, you've got to be faster on the track than they are, and the way to do that is by closing deals, attracting new business, and growing. With our reps and our company, it's activity, activity, activity. You've got to sell it. Surely there's more, but while the Hewlett-Packards and Dells of the world are big and bad, they're also pretty proud and they let customers come to them. We go get our customers.

One thing every entrepreneur should learn is that being told "no" by a banker, a client, or a prospect just means "not right now." There's no such thing as a "no."

With our reps and our company, it's activity, activity, activity. You've got to sell it.

•••

One thing every entrepreneur should learn is that being told "no" by a banker, a client, or a prospect just means "not right now." There's no such thing as a "no."

WHAT ARE YOUR READING HABITS?

I read industry trade magazines, the *National Business Journal*, the *Wall Street Journal*, and, at the end of the day, *Health & Fitness* magazine.

IF YOU WERE GOING TO WRITE A BOOK EITHER ABOUT YOUR COMPANY OR SOME OTHER PART OF YOUR LIFE, WHAT WOULD IT BE?

It wouldn't be about my company. My book would be about entrepreneurship, and it would be titled Corporate SOBs, which stands for "sons of business owners." Whether you're working for the man, a mom-and-pop, or a Fortune 500 company, all your bosses are SOBs, since everyone climbs a corporate ladder and the scenery is never going to change. You're always going to be looking up someone's rear. If you're working for a mom-and-pop, it's an SOB company. You're always going to be "looking up" if you're working there or if you're working for a huge company.

My book would be about entrepreneurship, and it would be titled Corporate SOBs, which stands for "sons of business owners."

•••

People have big ideas, but they don't know how to build a ship to get across the ocean.

My son said, "Daddy, I want to work for you one day."

I said, "No, you don't. You're not going to work for me, and you're not going to work for anyone else. You're going to work for yourself." I got an education to get the resume and get the interview. That's what you train for in college and everything else. No one's training you on how to run a business or start a business. America isn't making anything, and we're not training people in how to make businesses.

People have big ideas, but they don't know how to build a ship to get across the ocean.

Laurence Hallier

Show Media

LAURENCE HALLIER

FOUNDER AND CEO, SHOW MEDIA
NEW YORK, NEW YORK

Laurence Hallier – Show Media
Rank #6
3-Year % Growth: 11,749%
Revenue: $14.2 Million
Industry: Advertising & Marketing
# of Employees: 36
City/State: New York, NY

Show Media provides custom integrated advertising solutions to the country's largest companies, including Microsoft Bing, AT&T, Ray-Ban, HTC, Lionsgate Films, and other leaders in the beverage, liquor, banking, entertainment, retail, fashion, airline, and technology industries. The company's media properties range from traditional, out-of-home advertising to place-based networks designed to target specific audiences. Show Media also provides its brand partners with unique transportation-based campaigns in taxicabs and other livery vehicles.

YOUR GROWTH HAS BEEN ASTONISHING.

I don't know the exact number, but I think it's 11,500 percent, which is how we got to number 6 in 2011. Unfortunately, we hit that list three times in a row, and this year, it's hard. I think we're going to make it again, but not in the top 500. This will be our fourth year on the list.

That number definitely exceeded my expectations. It would kind of have to, right? I started probably thirty different businesses in the last 20 years. Every time I go into a business I always expect big things, and, knock on wood, I've been pretty successful at several of them. This one was much more challenging and much easier in some ways, just because I was getting back into a business I had been in for 15 years. The bad part is, we launched a year before October of 2008. We were launching our company in the middle of the economic downturn. Still, we've had tremendous growth that has exceeded my expectations.

I started probably thirty different businesses in the last 20 years. Every time I go into a business I always expect big things, and, knock on wood, I've been pretty successful at several of them.

WHAT MADE IT HAPPEN?

It's a combination of things. I believe that our team, our company or group of people who created this, is responsible in part. Obviously, leadership is important—that's me—but the team is as important. My philosophy is, "Have fun, make money." I believe philosophy starts at the top and goes all the way down, in that order, and we just stick to that. It's so simplistic, but it allows everybody to be on the same side of the fence. I've always said the product matters, but the team matters way more. I'd rather have a B- or a C-product with an A-team than have an A-product with a B-team all day long.

I think focus is important. We've had so many opportunities to do other things, but we focused on the core business and that worked, most importantly, for our advertisers. Leadership is important. I'm the captain, and I've got to keep the ship sailing in the right direction. I've got to keep my eye way ahead of the curve. I think sales, sales, sales. Our companies have always been driven in sales. Whether it's this advertising company or the real estate I did before, all my companies have been driven in sales.

My philosophy is, "Have fun, make money."

•••

I've always said the product matters, but the team matters way more. I'd rather have a B- or a C-product with an A-team than have an A-product with a B-team all day long.

•••

Leadership is important. I'm the captain, and I've got to keep the ship sailing in the right direction.

Forget the product. Your product may be the greatest thing in the world, but what does it do for the customer? Does it drive business? Does it increase the bottom line? We focus on that heavily, not just superficially. We don't rely on case studies that say, "Oh, our product and widget is great." How does it move the customers' needs? How does it sell more of their products and services? How does it achieve their goals for that quarter or for that year?

I think we're better than our competition, but overall I've been doing the same things for twenty years. We built the original advertising company and then built the second advertising company and sold it to Clear Channel. It was the same when I got into the real estate business and did a billion dollars in real estate in Nevada and Texas. I used the same principles.

For me, those principles have not changed. I've gotten better at them, I think. A couple of team members in this company were part of my real estate company before, and a couple of them were also part of my advertising company before that, in the '90s. They knew my philosophy. They're not new, but they're effective.

HOW DID YOU GET INTO THIS BUSINESS?

I got into this particular business by luck. I wanted to be a billionaire. I got into real estate. I took a lot of risks and saw some bad things coming down in late 2007. Then this opportunity came about. My old business was a taxi advertising business that my partner and I started in the early '90s. It was mostly tobacco and adult products and these old signs that we got involved in. We created that business in fourteen cities across the country.

In 2007, the mayor of New York mandated that credit cards go into cabs, and that gave us an opportunity to go in and sign up to 30 percent of the cabs to put the taxi tops on. At the time, we were heavily into real estate, and we decided, "Let's get back to my old business." Part of it was motivated by the fact that I felt real estate was on a bad path. (I never dreamed it would turn out as badly as it did.) That's how we got started. The company that had bought our taxi advertising company didn't want to take that opportunity, so we jumped back in.

We sold a portion of our business last year—the taxi tops, actually—to our biggest competitor, a company called VeriFone. We sold a chunk of our revenue, in part because they had 60 percent of the market in New York and we had 40 percent. One of us had to win, and we couldn't buy them, so we ended up selling to them. We got a good multiple, and it worked out great. About two years ago, we also launched heavily into digital space, so now we have digital screens in the back seats in Las Vegas taxis and in the black cars in New York. We had already launched that business, and we thought, "This is the future. It's all digital." It made sense to us.

A year from now, we're going to be up in revenue, which is pretty amazing because we sold about half of our revenue for the launch into the new digital. I think we're going to be even more profitable, which is great. More importantly, we're in a business that has unlimited growth. Before, we could sell only one taxi top to one advertiser, and now we can sell more than that. Now we have way more inventory. We'll cross $100 million in four years. We'll hit more than 5 times our current sales.

DO YOU EVEN HAVE COMPETITION?

Another philosophy of mine is that I like businesses that have a high margin and have some kind of unique—I hate the word monopoly—but some kind of unique product. Back to the taxi tops, we had competition, and it was difficult. We had developed a new top, and we were launching that; we knew that it would differentiate us from the competition. But, at the end of the day, it was difficult to compete toe-to-toe because we had the same product. Maybe ours was a little sexier, but it was still difficult. That problem's gone now because we sold it to our competitor and they've done well with the business.

We'll cross $100 million in four years. We'll hit more than 5 times our current sales.

•••

I like businesses that have a high margin and have some kind of unique—I hate the word monopoly—but some kind of unique product.

•••

Regarding the Las Vegas digital screens, we don't have a competitor, nor will we. We'll have the whole market.

Now we are focused on not having a competitor. Regarding the Las Vegas digital screens, we don't have a competitor, nor will we. We'll have the whole market. In New York black cars, we have the whole market too. We have 84 percent of the black car market, so there won't be a spot for someone to compete with us. I'd rather not have direct competition, but we obviously have competition. We fight for advertising dollars against elevator advertising, against coffee store advertising, and against all place-based media. So we certainly have competition. I just don't like competition that's in our space; otherwise, there's no benefit.

We're in New York, Los Angeles, and Las Vegas. We're headquartered in New York, and it's been great, actually. I worked in New York fifteen years ago and it seems like a better place to work than ever. I live in Los Angeles and Las Vegas. The company is based in New York because advertising is based in New York. All the ad agencies, all of the planning, and all of the buying services are based here. I shouldn't say "all," but close to 70 percent. Chicago has the rest of it. For us, being in New York has made total sense. We love New York. We think the pool of people is awesome. And I haven't always said that about New York. I think New York has become friendlier to business, especially small business.

To be successful, you have to have the best team, and the team has to be well motivated—not just motivated. Everybody has to be in it for the fun of it, not just to show up at a job. That's never going to work out. Company culture, to me, is everything, and it always has been. You might be the best salesperson in the world, but if you're a jerk, I don't care how good you are. I just don't care. You've got to have the attitude of, "Have fun, and then we're all going to make a lot of money."

Innovation is also important. That's clearly a big part of our company now, because we're in a digital space. Also, go fast and work hard. People forget that. In our company, everybody works until 8 at night. Everybody's motivated because they get that they're going to grow and learn something. When people are motivated, they love what they do, and that includes me. I think you do have to work hard. There's no getting around that. Give it everything you got. For real, really give it. Make all those calls. Wake up and work hard. Just give it all you've got, no matter who you are.

Company culture, to me, is everything, and it always has been.

•••

In our company, everybody works until 8 at night. Everybody's motivated because they get that they're going to grow and learn something.

•••

Really stretch yourself, grow, take chances, and develop skills.

WHAT'S A BOOK YOU LOVE?

I love Walter Isaacson's book on Steve Jobs. It's great because it shows you the Michael Jordan of business. We can all strive to be like that. I loved that book. I think it's awesome. I made all my people read it, and they all loved it.

If I ever wrote a book, it would be about going for it—in everything. In relationships, friends, and business, go for it. Give it all you've got. Live passionately. It sounds so clichéd, but you should actually do it. Really stretch yourself, grow, take chances, and develop skills.

Nick Chasinov

Teknicks

NICK CHASINOV

FOUNDER AND CEO, TEKNICKS
BAY HEAD, NEW JERSEY

Nick Chasinov – Tecknicks
Rank #163
3-Year % Growth: 1,797%
Revenue: $2 Million
Industry: Advertising & Marketing
# of Employees: 52
City/State: Bay Head, NJ

Teknicks is a young company that relies heavily on its relaxed office culture and bucolic campus for inspiration in the "interactive enhancement" field. The company provides search engine optimization, web design and development, pay-per-click advertising, social media, e-mail marketing, mobile marketing, reputation management, and web analytics. Teknicks has launched campaigns for some of the world's largest brands, including MTV, McGraw-Hill publishing, *Elle*, Bloomberg, *Car and Driver*, and Brookstone.

WHERE ARE YOU LOCATED AND WHY?

Where we are located plays a huge role in the success of our company. We are in Bay Head, New Jersey, so we're actually at the Jersey Shore, about an hour outside of Philadelphia, depending on how you drive. I think the city of Bay Head has tremendously impacted our business.

We sit on Twilight Lake, and we're one block from the beach. We actually have a waterfront courtyard, and we have picnic tables and a barbecue and plenty of room for creativity. We were just voted the fourth best place to work in New Jersey, and we know the city of Bay Head, our actual location, and our campus have come together and provided an incubator for innovation. I'm confident the city has impacted us positively.

We were just voted the fourth best place to work in New Jersey, and we know the city of Bay Head, our actual location, and our campus have come together and provided an incubator for innovation.

Sure, we could conduct our business from anywhere, but what interests me is quality of life, or at least quality of work life. There's a saltwater lake in our backyard. It's a calm, brackish lake, and our courtyard is right there; we have a private, huge lot, and it's an amazing place. Actually, I feel as though the place chose us. We grew out of our first space in a year, and we were looking for an office that represented our culture.

HOW DID YOU FIND IT?

Our sales agent came across this large waterfront lot that had two buildings and a private courtyard, and we immediately knew we had something special. We needed to do a little bit of construction, but nothing drastic. I remember holding our first staff meeting outside, at the picnic tables. We all just looked at each other and said, "This is great. It doesn't even feel like work." People want to come here; they want to create great things and be innovative. I think our physical work environment helps support positive output.

We have grown 136 percent over the last three years. We set the bar high, so we were extremely pleased with our three-year growth rate. However, I think the bigger story for us, and the thing that exceeded our expectations, was our four-year growth rate of 726 percent. When we look at our evolution over the last three or four years, we're extremely pleased.

I remember holding our first staff meeting outside, at the picnic tables. We all just looked at each other and said, "This is great. It doesn't even feel like work."

•••

What's been helpful for us is the fact that we're ranked number one on Google for a lot of our services.

Then again, we shouldn't be surprised because we practice what we preach. We're an SEO agency, so we get paid to make sure our clients and their websites are ranked on Google. What's been helpful for us is the fact that we're ranked number one on Google for a lot of our services. This ranking validates our ability to execute successful, world-class search engine marketing programs, and it gives people reassurance. That's been a key component to our growth.

WHAT ELSE?

Our portfolio and proof of concepts have also helped. Our approach to selling has always been to show people tangible examples. We have a tremendous amount of number-one Google rankings that we have secured for companies in a wide range of industries, and we're able to show this in our sales presentation and in our pitches. That has been a great way to generate new leads.

One thing we strictly enforce is our merited approach and ethical methodology regarding SEO, which is respected in the industry. We promote adherence to Google guidelines. Our prospects appreciate that and know we're always going to be suggesting marketing tactics and technology that are in line with best practices. They know there's nothing they need to worry about. I think that's also been a key driver of our growth; another driver is our dedicated staff. Our staff has been tremendous. They care just as much about our clients' performance as their own, and in the services industry, client management is everything.

Innovation has also helped us grow. We're constantly deploying new technologies, techniques, and strategies, adapting to both algorithm changes in the search engines and general advances in the market and the Internet. Right now, we're in the middle of a transformation in the way the Internet is being used with Facebook and other social platforms. Our programs embrace that change in an ethical manner, and that has also helped us grow. It's safe to say these practices have been in place all along at our company, but we've adapted to the industry's evolution. So, what worked twelve months ago is not working any longer. We're always adapting, but these ideas have been in place at the company's core since the beginning. We've been following them for the full eight years we've been in business.

One thing we strictly enforce is our merited approach and ethical methodology regarding SEO, which is respected in the industry.

•••

We're constantly deploying new technologies, techniques, and strategies, adapting to both algorithm changes in the search engines and general advances in the market and the Internet.

I began making websites in my early twenties, and 2004 was a perfect time to start the company. Facebook had emerged, and there were a lot of other things going on in the industry. I was twenty-three. I thought it was clear that web design and Internet marketing were in demand, so I joined a local chapter of a business networking organization. I closed a web design deal at the first meeting and Teknicks was born. That day, I knew that it was going to work.

WHAT DOES THE FUTURE LOOK LIKE?

Today, we think of Teknicks as an interactive enhancement agency. I think in a year we're going to think of it as an international interactive enhancement agency, and we're going to have several new divisions. In four years, I see Teknicks being one of the most innovative interactive enhancement agencies in existence, providing world-class digital marketing solutions while still developing proprietary technologies that will drive actionable insights into some of the most well-known brands.

Our strategies and marketing programs continue to yield industry-leading results year after year, and we evolve our services to adapt to the changes occurring in the industry. We're client-centric and our model is based on customer performance; I think our competitors are primarily traditional agencies focused on themselves. We also understand the relationship between growth and client performance, and I think that approach has proven to be reliable and scalable. We're seeing a shift in the marketplace, a shift away from the old style of marketing. Madison Avenue agencies and many of our competitors are just not acceptable any more.

///

Madison Avenue agencies and many of our competitors are just not acceptable any more.

///

WHY NOT?

It all comes down to performance and results for our clients, but I think a key component to that is measurement—relatable proof. You need to be able to provide data and reports beyond just what everyone can get from an out-of-the-box analytics tool. Our team is certified in Google Analytics, and we deliver actionable insights, not just reports, to our clients. Clients and brands are spending so much money online that they're seeing a shift in accountability from the old agency way of doing business, from the "What exactly are we delivering to you?" mentality, that is presented in just an Excel spreadsheet or a PDF. If you are a client of ours, we offer you actionable insights that tell you how you can better spend your marketing budget and attract the demographic you're targeting.

No one else is doing it the way we do it, and that's been a key to our success. We're actually changing the game, and now other agencies are taking notice and being accountable for this. We all talk and the people from the big brands sit on the same boards, and we're seeing a shift in accountability. Clearly, measurement and that type of technology are having an impact.

//

We're actually changing the game, and now other agencies are taking notice and being accountable for this.

//

Those are the biggest lessons for entrepreneurs in our industry. For entrepreneurs in any industry, the biggest lesson is the simplest one: get your books in order and have a good accountant. We've experienced moments in which things could have gotten on the wrong track for us if we were not properly organized, but, luckily, we have always been in good shape. We've made sure to have a good fiscal policy in place and a good accountant.

//

For entrepreneurs in any industry, the biggest lesson is the simplest one: get your books in order and have a good accountant.

//

I read a lot, but the few key resources I go to every day are Google News, Bloomberg, and several industry-related websites and blogs. If you're at a startup company, which means you're the CEO and the salesman, then I recommend you read *Mr. Shmooze: The Art and Science of Selling Through Relationships* by Richard Abraham. It provides great tactics and ideas that any business owner or salesman can implement. It's all about how to sell through relationships. It's a great, short read. If you worked at my company, you could read it over several lunch hours, sitting outside on the shores of Twilight Lake.

Noah Leask

ISHPI

NOAH LEASK

CO-FOUNDER, CHAIRMAN, CEO, AND PRESIDENT, ISHPI

MT. PLEASANT, SOUTH CAROLINA

Noah Leask – ISHPI

Rank #304

3-Year % Growth: 1,081%

Revenue: $5.6 Million

Industry: Government Services

# of Employees: 65

City/State: Mount Pleasant, SC

ISHPI is a military contracting firm that offers its clients a broad range of fully integrated information and cyber dominance services with core capabilities in information operations, information warfare, information assurance, electronic warfare, cybersecurity, and cyberwarfare. ISHPI, which also offers C5ISR [Command, Control, Communications, Computers, Combat Systems, Intelligence, Surveillance, and Reconnaissance] engineering and technical services, has capabilities in system engineering and integration, intelligence support, enterprise architecture, acquisition management, logistics support, training, and information technology. *ISHPI* teams work closely with clients to create business and technology solutions for intelligence community organizations, the Department of Defense, the Department of Homeland Security, federal agencies, and the commercial sector.

Our three-year growth rate is quite low compared to our five-year growth rate of 1,215 percent. Our three-year growth rate did not meet our expectations. We hit a plateau in 2009 due to a major catastrophe late in that year, when we lost 68.5 percent of our booked revenue going into 2010. We are now fully recovered. Overall, our five-year growth is pretty outstanding.

HOW DID YOU DO THAT?

We did it by adhering to five simple concepts: dedication, integrity, hard work, putting in long hours, and fielding the right team. None of those are new ideas, but it has been tremendously challenging to locate and field the right team.

In 2009, we had grown tremendously, reaching $5.9 million, up from $1.9 million in 2008. We grew the overhead to match by hiring the staff it takes to support that level of revenue. And then we reached the end of 2009 and found out we were once again a $2 million company. We acted quickly, convening my senior management, and two things became clear: one, we did not have the robust business development and sales pipeline to rapidly recover from the situation; and two, we didn't have the right team. It is critical to learn how to put the right team together and get out of their way so they can be successful. Let go and grow.

It is critical to learn how to put the right team together and get out of their way so they can be successful. Let go and grow.

We did have some of the pieces, but we were missing the vital pipeline and intimate customer relationships we needed. I had to make the hard decision to let some of the team go, but we also made a great strategic hire: our vice president of corporate development. We focused on becoming a strong company known for delivering our clients' missions. We also focused on becoming a competitive prime contractor in the government space. We knew it would take nine months to two years, so my wife and I had to be prepared to make the investments required to get there. We did it, but it was not easy.

By April of 2011, we had won our first competitive contract award. We won our second in June and several more in September. By the end of 2011, ISHPI had doubled. We have already realized more revenue in the first six months of 2012 than we did in all of 2011.

WHY DID YOU CHOOSE THIS KIND OF BUSINESS?

One reason was we knew we could do it right with ethics and integrity. Another reason was that I could live and work in Charleston, South Carolina. Charleston has a great culture and quality of life. It's not hard to get people to come here and stay for work. Also, it has a great airport that can easily get me to where I need to go nationwide. We love the Charleston area. This is where my wife and I want to be, and where we want to raise our kids.

HOW DO THINGS LOOK, GOING FORWARD?

ISHPI has become a highly sought-after company known for delivering our client's missions. We have a major focus in information and cyber dominance, and we have strong capabilities in Command, Control, Communications, Computers, Combat Systems, Intelligence, Surveillance, and Reconnaissance (C5ISR) engineering and technical services. We have expanded to nearly one hundred employees, providing services coast-to-coast, and in Alaska and Hawaii.

In a year, we will have more than one hundred and sixty employees and conduct 85 percent of our work in the position of prime contractor. We will be working for all of the major cyber clients in the Department of Defense, the Department of Homeland Security, and the intelligence community. We will also have entered into other federal agencies, such as the Department of Energy, the Department of State, the Department of Corrections, the Department of Transportation, and others, providing our vital network security operations and cyber defense services. In four years, we will be known for innovative research and development that will have contributed to the United States' continued information superiority, and revenues from that R&D should exceed $250 million per year.

I wouldn't say we are outrunning our competitors, but we are winning work using the lessons of the past and the solid business development and capture processes we have built, in addition to delivering the clients' missions. The key to success is performing well. You have only one chance to show a customer you were the right choice. Blowing it can have a tremendous negative impact on your reputation, which will make it hard to win future work.

You have only one chance to show a customer you were the right choice.

WHAT DO YOU READ?

I read for pleasure prior to going to bed nightly, but for work I read online throughout the day, checking in on Fox News, Fox Business, FedBizOpps, Defense.gov, Washington Technology, *Inc.*, and *Entrepreneur*. A book everyone should read is *Good to Great: Why Some Companies Make the Leap…and Others Don't* by Jim Collins. There are some great lessons in there, like having your team "on the bus." That seems easy, but it is critical, and hard to do.

And if I were to write a book, I would want to write *Government Contracting for Dummies.*

Reddy Annappareddy

Pharmacare

REDDY ANNAPPAREDDY

FOUNDER, PHARMACARE
BEL AIR, MARYLAND

Reddy Annappareddy – Pharmacare
Rank #364
3-Year % Growth: 937%
Revenue: $18 Million
Industry: Health
# of Employees: 36
City/State: Baltimore, MD

Reddy Annappareddy founded Pharmacare, an independent pharmacy chain based in the Baltimore, Maryland, area, in 2006. The tiny community pharmacy had to compete against twenty-five major chain pharmacies within a five-mile radius. Not only did it survive, it also became one of the fastest-growing specialty network pharmacies in the region. This resulted in Annappareddy winning the prestigious Ernst & Young Entrepreneur of the Year award in 2010. The national honor was validation for a company that stuck to its principles and offered a quality service at a reasonable price, all while resurrecting the time-honored practice of door-to-door delivery.

Our growth rate in the last three years was around 670 percent. We started in 2006, so it surprised us until 2008 and 2009, but after that we began to expect it. We have kept our bar so high that it's no longer surprising to us.

HOW ARE YOU KEEPING THE BAR HIGH?

Customer service is number one. We wanted to provide a lot of good services that no one else was providing. And savings. We're trying to provide the customers with some kind of savings, whether it's value in terms of money or in terms of services they can put some monetary value on. Another way is through employee benefits. We're trying to share our good fortune with our employees so we can encourage them and inspire them. A good management team is always a great asset because you cannot do anything on your own. Finally, you need good partnerships—with your bank, or your wholesaler, or whomever you partner with on a daily basis—to make sure you get things done.

We're trying to share our good fortune with our employees so we can encourage them and inspire them.

HAVE YOU TWEAKED THOSE IDEAS THROUGH THE YEARS?

I changed our business plan the fourth day we were in business. Customer service, savings, employee loyalty, a good management team, and good partnerships—none of that was in the original business plan. The original plan was to be a mom-and-pop pharmacy. Pharmacare started as a small business. However, I did not know the importance of the location at that time. I happened to choose the worst location in my city. It's a small town. We have 25 pharmacies in a five-mile radius. Mine is in the worst location, so I didn't have any customers for four days. I had to change the whole plan.

I changed our business plan the fourth day we were in business.

•••

When we followed the original plan and customers didn't come to us, I decided we should go to the customers.

•••

However, we did almost $50 million in aggregate sales in 2011. We changed everything after we started the business.

When we followed the original plan and customers didn't come to us, I decided we should go to the customers. To go to the customers, we had to select which customers we should target, so we came up with a completely different business model, which helped get us to where we are today. The original business plan projections were to make $3.8

million in 2011. However, we did almost $50 million in aggregate sales in 2011. We changed everything after we started the business.

Before I founded Pharmacare, I wanted to be on my own for a long time. However, I didn't have the money. I didn't have any means, so I never had the option of opening my own business. I was working for Rite Aid. I had all of these ideas about how to increase Rite Aid sales. I wrote about seventy plans, describing different ways we could do it. I drove to Rite Aid corporate headquarters and gave an executive the plan. The guy who happened to receive it was the vice president of some department. He trashed my idea, saying that I should not be doing his job, and he told me to go and do my job.

That gave me some inspiration. I worked like a dog for the next five years to make some money, so I could start my own business and I did. One thing I learned during those days is that I'm in the service industry. I learned how to take care of a customer, and that is the core of our business: customer service.

I'm in the service industry. I learned how to take care of a customer, and that is the core of our business: customer service.

Today, we are in Maryland, D.C., Pennsylvania, and North Carolina. We are doing approximately $55 million in aggregate sales. We hope to do $100 million by the end of this year. If we hit $100 million this year, we will be doing approximately $20 million a month by December of 2013, which is going to put us at the $250 million mark. In four years, I want Pharmacare to be at least a $500 million company. That is what we are working toward. We might not be able to do it, but at least we have a goal and we are working toward it.

HOW DO YOU STAY FOCUSED?

Whether people agree with this or not, the healthcare sector is passion-driven. You have to have passion. Sometimes you drive five hours for a customer in order to deliver a $4 medication. When you promise a free home delivery, you don't look for money. Even then, if you enjoy what you are doing, that's passion. We do that to the core. Our goal is to take care of our customers, and we enjoy every step, even if we lose money in some transactions. We never pay attention to the money. Even though money is the primary thing, healthcare is a different business. I have a clear advantage because I call the shots. Rite Aid says, "It's $4. We don't do home delivery." Right there, that's one of our biggest advantages.

Sometimes you drive five hours for a customer in order to deliver a $4 medication.

•••

Our goal is to take care of our customers, and we enjoy every step, even if we lose money in some transactions.

Since we go to the patients, the city we are in does not affect our current business model. We are trying to be careful in selecting nice locations whenever we expand. It's definitely part of the equation, but it's not the only question. We are in several states and several cities right now, including D.C. I just bought a business in Detroit for the company, and we are buying one in Texas. We are a multi-state business, so now we are beyond the importance of location. Right now, we base our whole business out of Baltimore, which is my home city. I have been living in Maryland for the last eighteen years. I have every reason to contribute to the Maryland economy, and this is where we started.

WHAT'S YOUR ADVICE TO ASPIRING ENTREPRENEURS?

A, follow your heart. If you think you are going to do it, do it. Come up with a plan, and don't wait for somebody to come and help you. You should start doing it today; eventually, help will come to you in some way. You shouldn't worry about it. B, don't take anything personally, and don't fall in love with your ideas. You should not say, "Oh, I *have* to do this." You should not drive your business compulsively. If there is growth, there will be pain. Follow whatever the right thing to do is, but don't follow because you think you have to do it. And don't let your ego or personal attitude affect your business. You have to be a real businessman to be successful.

Don't take anything personally, and don't fall in love with your ideas.

•••

If there is growth, there will be pain.

WHAT DO YOU LIKE TO READ?

I love the *New York Times*, and I read it every day. Without reading the *Times* and without going to CNN (of course, everything is online), I don't start my day. At the end of the day, when I come home, around 8 or sometimes 10 in the evening, I try to wind down. I process data for half an hour, have a Scotch, and then find a spot where I can read, look at the newspaper, and get the latest news, and then I go to bed.

I have a couple of business books that I like, but out of all books, the one I would recommend is called *Who Moved My Cheese?: A Way to Deal with Changing Your Work and Your Life* by Spencer Johnson. It's a small book, maybe thirty pages, which I first read a long time ago. It's a good book. I recommend all entrepreneurs read it because it will change the way they think about certain things.

NPR did a thirty-minute segment on me as one of the most inspiring individuals in the United States. They aired it, and then the Kauffman Foundation and *Inc.* magazine did these nice articles on me. I think a lot of people helped motivate me to get where I am today. So if I were going to write a book, I would try to motivate other people. My book would be called, *If I Can Do It, Why Can't You Do It?*

I came to this country with almost nothing, just $4,000 to pay my tuition. Eighteen years down the road, I contribute a lot to the economy by running a company of 120 full-time employees. We donate approximately $500,000 to charities every year. If I can do it with nothing, someone who was born in this country can do it one hundred times better than I have.

If I can do it with nothing, someone who was born in this country can do it one hundred times better than I have.

Vicky Thompson

Valuation Management Group

VICKY THOMPSON

PRESIDENT AND CEO, VALUATION MANAGEMENT GROUP
MARIETTA, GEORGIA

Vicky Thompson – Valuation
Management Group
Rank #22
3-Year % Growth: 7,910%
Revenue: $25.4 Million
Industry: Real Estate
# of Employees: 50
City/State: Marietta, GA

Real estate appraisal veteran Vicky Thompson leads the Valuation Management Group (VMG), a nationwide commercial and residential appraisal management company that serves community banks, mortgage bankers, credit unions, and wholesale lenders. VMG handles the entire appraisal process, including approving appraisers, managing the appraiser panel, handling the bid process on complex residential properties and commercial assignments, ordering environmental risk assessments, engaging the appraisers, and performing a quality appraisal review. More than half of the company's appraisers have close to twenty years of experience in the business. This, along with a strong set of ethics, has set VMG apart.

TELL US ABOUT YOUR GROWTH.

Our growth rate was 6,267 percent, and that significantly exceeded any expectations we had or even our notions of what was possible. We had no idea we could do that. Some of the things that helped us get there were working in the changed lending environment and being aware of real estate values. Other factors were regulatory change, which required greater independence, and reviews based on the real estate debacle—the decline in values as well as the original over-valuing of appraised values.

In addition, our business is different from our competition in that we listened to our clients' needs, built our company to support them, and have true independence. It's more like a partnership with them, an outsourced opportunity that is part of their bank, mortgage bank, or credit union. One of the important things is that 99 percent of our business comes from referrals. We do very little marketing or sales. Also, our staff is far more experienced than our competitors' staff: more than half of our employees have close to twenty years of experience.

Our growth rate was 6,267 percent, and that significantly exceeded any expectations we had or even our notions of what was possible.

•••

We listen to our clients' needs, built our company to support them, and have true independence.

ARE ANY OF THESE IDEAS NEW?

These ideas evolved based on our original business plan. We had a business plan and a structure that was different from that of other appraisal management companies, but, as the market has changed, we have evolved with it. Our basic business model hasn't changed, but we've evolved as the environment has changed.

I had a traditional appraisal company I had started in 1993, and in 2005 I bought another appraisal company. I merged the two together, and I probably paid way too much for it, because it was at the height of the market. Once I purchased the second company, the refis and purchases all started slowing down significantly. I was feeling the impact, and I was probably a little bit ahead of other appraisal firms. Based on that, and the need to survive, I said, "Wait a minute. We're going to have to do something different." I started the new company thinking there was a need for appraiser independence. But clients still wanted to use the appraisers they were familiar with, so we had to reinvent the process. That was in 2006.

///

I said, "Wait a minute. We're going to have to do something different."

///

Our business is a vibrant, exciting company with an excellent staff that we want to continue to grow without compromising our commitment to client satisfaction. Currently, we are reorganizing our processes and procedures based on our growth and our opportunity for extreme growth in the near future. We're increasing our staff, and in a year we expect to have grown by 25 percent. Percentage-wise, that is small in comparison to our past three years. But once you get to a certain size, the percentages result in bigger and bigger actual numbers. In four years, we expect to be a $100 million company. Last year we were about a $35 million company.

WHAT SETS YOU APART FROM YOUR COMPETITION?

I believe it's our reputation, our strong ethics, and our experienced, knowledgeable staff. None of our competitors can say that 52 percent of their staff, those who are appraisers, have more than eighteen years of experience. Most of them go out and try to hire the cheapest person they can find to do a job or fill a position. We look at it a little differently because we do consider ourselves partners with our clients. Obviously, we want to be profitable, and we are. But that's not our ultimate goal. Our ultimate goal is to provide a service to our clients. We're in Atlanta, which is a progressive city with talented professionals. However, the depressed job market, especially in real estate in Atlanta, has made it possible for us to enlist great human capital. From the day we started through our most recent round of hiring, we've been able to pull from a great pool of talent right in Atlanta. I've lived here since 1989, and I love the city. I would never have considered moving. We are a national company, and with Atlanta's airports and direct flights it's easy to get anywhere we need to.

I think one of the keys to our success has been our commitment to our clients' partners. They trust us, and they're comfortable referring us. We take care of them, and they are comfortable knowing that when they refer us to someone else, their own service is not going to be diminished. And they know we will do a good job for whomever they refer us to and that makes them look good, too.

WHAT LESSON SHOULD EVERY ENTREPRENEUR LEARN?

The number one thing is, when you think you cannot do something for a client, you say, "Yeah, we can do it, but let's figure out how we can do it." Even with my traditional firm, when I was researching going into business, I talked to thirteen people and they said, "No, you don't want to do it." I did it anyway and was successful, and the same thing happened in 2006 with the appraisal management company. Everybody thought it was a crazy idea. One of my current clients, whose wife happens to work for me, said to me recently, "You know, when you used to call on me and try to sell me this idea, I thought it was the stupidest thing I'd ever heard." He went on to admit, "But now I'm just amazed at your success and what you've been able to do."

The number one thing is, when you think you cannot do something for a client, you say, "Yeah, we can do it, but let's figure out how we can do it."

WHERE DO YOU GET YOUR INFORMATION?

I get a lot of daily industry e-mail—news, links, papers, and periodicals—off the Internet. That's pretty much my daily routine: Internet and e-mail for about an hour or an hour and a half every morning. As for a book, I recommend a simple classic, *Rich Dad, Poor Dad*, by Robert Kiyosaki. I recently reread it. I grew up in a poor family and only had a high school education. My dad didn't work regularly, and we didn't have any financial or business training, or any of those basics. To me, this book tells readers, "Hey, you can do it, but you've got to pay attention, and you have to have the courage to do it." It fits everybody, from an eighteen-year-old forward to any age.

I grew up in a poor family and only had a high school education.

If I wrote a book of my own, it would be titled, *Always Say No First, but Never Accept No*. When my employees come to me, most of the time I tell them, "I don't think you can do it that way. Prove to me how you can." I effectively say no, but then I ask them to tell me why and how they could succeed, and I make sure they're committed to it. However, I never accept no, and neither should they.

Josef Gorowitz

Prodege

JOSEF GOROWITZ

FOUNDER AND CEO, PRODEGE
TORRANCE, CALIFORNIA

Josef Gorowitz – Prodege
Rank #43
3-Year % Growth: 4,461%
Revenue: $12.3 Million
Industry: Advertising & Marketing
# of Employees: 25
City/State: Torrance, CA

Prodege is the world's leading creator of online rewards programs. The company has developed more than one hundred fifty such programs, including the Internet's most popular rewards program and destination, Swagbucks.com. This program enables users to earn virtual currency that can be redeemed for real-life rewards simply by engaging in everyday activity on the Internet. The activity can include anything from searching the Web to playing games or shopping online. Prodege also runs a network of branded rewards portals for some of the most popular brands in the world, including WWE, KISS, the Green Bay Packers, and *Star Trek*.

Our growth rate was 4,461 percent. I didn't run the business in a way in which we put this projection in place and tried to hit it. It was an evolving business, and our growth definitely did not happen at once, where it surprised us. There were no expectations going into it, so I can't say we were following any kind of blueprint.

SO TO WHAT DO YOU ATTRIBUTE IT?

It all stems from investing in personnel, taking the risk to bring on smart, hard-working, and qualified people. With every employee that we brought on—we went from one, which was just myself, to about fifty-five—we felt we were adding more value to our company. Our people were helping our product get out in the marketplace; they were optimizing our product. Sometimes we did not know exactly what value they were adding to our company, but we trusted and empowered the people around us, and it made a huge difference.

With every employee that we brought on—we went from one, which was just myself, to about fifty-five—we felt we were adding more value to our company.

•••

Another big thing, and part of our success, is that we have been careful not to grow in a way in which our customers get hurt.

Another big thing, and part of our success, is that we have been careful not to grow in a way in which our customers get hurt. You can enjoy this incredible growth, but if you're hurting your customers by promising things you can't deliver, then right away you're going to flatten out. We were always careful, especially in our rewards program. Any rewards program that promises a reward and does not come through is obviously going to be out of business quickly. You might have had some kind of escalated activity because you fooled somebody and promised a new TV or something, but in our case we made sure we did not offer big promises. We were not giving away millions of dollars at a time. We gave out one dollar at a time, and we made sure we were able to pay it off quickly. Being true to our customers has been important to us.

///

The demographic was stay-at-home moms. We've connected well with the mommy bloggers who write about money-saving opportunities, or coupons, and we incentivized and rewarded them for letting their communities know about our product.

///

We came out with a product that served the masses, but we targeted a certain demographic and got the leaders and connectors within that demographic to help us spread the word. The demographic was stay-at-home moms. We've connected well with the mommy bloggers who write about money-saving opportunities, or coupons, and we incentivized and rewarded them for letting their communities know about our product. So we found a niche, started building our base there, and then were able to expand to the masses.

To go after a niche and focus on building with the leaders in that community, partnering with them; that was a new idea. Being true to the customer and building a great team was an idea I had from day one. We knew if we were going to be successful we needed to do it that way.

WHY DID YOU PICK THIS TYPE OF BUSINESS?

This is the second business I've started. The first, in 2005, was an export company out of Argentina that shipped 44,000-pound containers around the world. It was a different business than what we're doing now. I had a partner in the business and was not a day-to-day manager, but I felt the stress of a day-to-day manager. Google had their big IPO, and I felt that was the first time when monetization of the web became real. People were actually earning revenue from activities online, and it intrigued me that Google could make all of that money while people were at home on their computers, just doing a simple click here and there. It was different than shipping containers around the world. I decided I wanted to get into web monetization and web e-commerce.

Today, our business continues to grow. Our rewards community continues to grow in numbers, and our rewards opportunities continue to grow. The years 2011 and 2010 continued our 100 percent growth trend. We are expecting 2012 to be north of 65 percent growth over 2011. We plan to expand and take our product internationally, moving it onto other platforms, such as mobile devices and tablets. There are some competitors that are with us as far as the growth goes, but most of our competitors started about seven to ten years ago, and at this point they're pretty flat. We built a more fun, exciting social brand.

We're plugged into social media. We have a Facebook page with more than a million likes, and that is where we have access to our users. These types of things, while growing, give us the advantage of being more current. We are in Torrance, California. I would not say it has affected us one way or the other. We're an online business, so we don't service the local community per se. We service the online base. I was living here when I started the business. That's the only reason we're here.

We're an online business, so we don't service the local community per se. We service the online base.

•••

You have to promise, but you have to make sure you come through. In addition to coming through, you need to shock consumers and surprise them at how well you've come through.

The key to being successful in our business is being honest to the consumer and not over-promising. It's better to under-promise and over-deliver. The rewards program industry has had shysters who have taken advantage of consumers by promising them rewards and not following through. If you want to be successful in this industry, you have to do the opposite. You have to promise, but you have to make sure you come through. In addition to coming through, you need to shock consumers and surprise them at how well you've come through. Being honest and transparent, even to the level where it might hurt the bottom line or the top line in the moment, is the only way to build sustainability in the online loyalty business.

Entrepreneurs need to learn, or remember, that they are not the only entrepreneurs involved. An entrepreneur is only an entrepreneur if he surrounds himself with other entrepreneurs. An entrepreneur needs to create other entrepreneurs, many of them, and together they can all be successful. One person can't do it all. You have to trust and empower other people around you.

///

Entrepreneurs need to learn, or remember, that they are not the only entrepreneurs involved.

///

WHAT DO YOU LIKE TO READ?

All of my daily reading is online. I also pray every day. That's important. Three times a day, actually, I pray. I read Tech Crunch, the Huffington Post, the Drudge Report, and All Things Digital. Those are the things I do on a daily basis. I think everyone should read *Good to Great: Why Some Companies Make the Leap…and Others Don't* by Jim Collins. It is a study of ten successful companies and ten comparable companies that went off the cliff. The book explains the common denominator in each case, and what the ten successful companies did. It shares lessons that every entrepreneur could learn from and should apply to his or her company.

If I were to write a book of my own, it would be about how to use entrepreneurship both in business and in everyday life. It would be about how to become a better family man, which would result in having a better family, a better community, and a better society.

YOU THINK IT'S ALL CONNECTED?

Yep. You can't be one way in the office, a different way at home, and a different way when on vacation. There's one method you have to carry through. If it's all in sync, you can do a lot.

You can't be one way in the office, a different way at home, and a different way when on vacation.

EPILOGUE

Amazing, right? I hope you got as much out of these stories as I did. Our goal for this book, all along, was to collect and distribute the wisdom of these successful, motivated, and intellectually curious people, and perhaps to inspire you, the reader, to innovate within your own business or rejuvenate some part of your life.

Even if you are not a business professional trying to start or grow a company, how could you not be inspired by Laurence Hallier's challenge to do everything in life with purpose and passion? "In relationships, friends, and business, go for it," you might recall him saying. "Give it all you've got. Live passionately. It sounds so clichéd, but you should actually do it. Really stretch yourself, grow, take chances, and develop skills."

Getting going, and keeping going, is often the hardest part. Every now and then, we need a boost, a pat on the back, or a kick in the pants—something to remind us the journey is worth taking and everyone else is taking it with us at the exact same time. Some of these people have figured out a better route than others, and we look to those wise and experienced folks for clues, in books such as this one, about how to make our own businesses and lives better.

Getting going, and keeping going, is often the hardest part. Every now and then, we need a boost, a pat on the back, or a kick in the pants.

I believe books written by entrepreneurs about businesses and entrepreneurship are important because they allow us into a world to which we were not previously privy—a world that is inhabited by some of the greatest business minds of all time. For just $20, the price of a book, we can get into the mind of Walt Disney, Albert Einstein, Steve Jobs, or Andrew Grove, one of Intel's co-founders. It's incredible. You can get an "MBA" for a couple hundred dollars just by buying and reading great books.

The most successful entrepreneurs I have observed are typically the most open-minded people. They are open to new ideas, and they are excited to be continuously learning. They are connoisseurs of information, always looking for ideas to make their organizations better. If you, as an entrepreneur, do not have that attitude, you will have trouble growing your business.

Every single day, the economy is changing, technology is changing, and consumers' habits are changing. As all of these things change, new needs crop up. Then again, needs that exist today may not exist tomorrow. Just ten years ago, people needed cameras and film. Then, for most Americans, Steve Jobs eliminated that need. Now, if you buy an iPhone, you certainly do not need to buy film. Chances are you may never buy a digital camera again; your cell phone has such a high-quality picture-taking ability you have no need to buy another device.

As an entrepreneur, if you are not constantly observing all of these changes and gaining insight from the thought leaders who are helping orchestrate these changes—if you are not paying attention, if you are not continually learning— you are going to get left behind. This does not mean you will be the last one to make it to the dinner trough. It means that you will go out of business. I think entrepreneurs, probably more than people in any other profession, always need to be learning, adapting, and paying attention to what is going on in the market.

Entrepreneurs, probably more than people in any other profession, always need to be learning, adapting, and paying attention to what is going on in the market.

If I could, would I do things differently with my own business? Sure. For the most part, I am happy with where I am. That said, if I could do it over again, I would spend even more time than I did reading and learning. I would spend more time learning to be a better leader. When I say "leader," I mean a person who both has a great idea and is able to communicate that great idea, and who is caring, nurturing, and fun loving. A *real* leader.

This book is filled with the thoughts of real leaders, and I hope you have taken as much from it as I have. As I said in the Introduction, I hope your copy is now filled with notes and comments in the margins. I hope you will return to this book again and again on your journey. I know I will.

I also hope you share this book with people you care about—people you want to inspire, mentor, or entertain. The exchange of ideas is the highest calling we have as businesspeople and human beings. If this book has taught you something, caused you to wonder about a topic, or simply reaffirmed your belief in the value of your life's work and your journey, it has done its job.

Thank you for reading our work.

Sincerely,

Adam Witty, CEO
Advantage Media Group
awitty@advantageww.com
advantagefamily.com

How can you use this book?

MOTIVATE

EDUCATE

THANK

INSPIRE

PROMOTE

CONNECT

Why have a custom version of *Secrets of the Inc. 500*?

- Build personal bonds with customers, prospects, employees, donors, and key constituencies
- Develop a long-lasting reminder of your event, milestone, or celebration
- Provide a keepsake that inspires change in behavior and change in lives
- Deliver the ultimate "thank you" gift that remains on coffee tables and bookshelves
- Generate the "wow" factor

Books are thoughtful gifts that provide a genuine sentiment that other promotional items cannot express. They promote employee discussions and interaction, reinforce an event's meaning or location, and they make a lasting impression. Use your book to say "Thank You" and show people that you care.

www.ingramcontent.com/pod-product-compliance
Lightning Source LLC
Chambersburg PA
CBHW051513170526
45165CB00002B/454